KEEPING
KIDS OUT OF
THE MIDDLE

Child-Centered Parenting in the Midst
of Conflict, Separation, and Divorce

BENJAMIN D. GARBER, PH.D.
Founder of HealthyParent.com

Health Communications, Inc.
Deerfield Beach, Florida

www.hcibooks.com

Disclaimer: This book provides general advice. It is not intended as a substitute for consultation with a trusted child-centered professional.

Library of Congress Cataloging-in-Publication Data

Garber, Benjamin D. (Benjamin David), 1959–
    Keeping kids out of the middle : child-centered parenting in the midst of adult conflict, separation, and divorce / Benjamin D. Garber.
        p. cm.
    Includes index.
    ISBN-13: 978-0-7573-0711-9 (trade paper)
    ISBN-10: 0-7573-0711-6 (trade paper)
        1. Parenting, Part-time.   2.Children of divorced parents.   3. Divorced parents.
I. Title.
    HQ755.8.G35 2008
    306.874—dc22

                                                                    2008022746

Publisher: Health Communications, Inc.
            3201 S.W. 15th Street
            Deerfield Beach, FL 33442-8190

Cover design by Justin Rotkowitz
Interior formatting by Dawn Von Strolley Grove

This book is dedicated to Mollie, Zoe, and Laura and to all families who struggle to put their children's needs first.

I am indebted to Janice Pieroni of Story Arts Management (Boston) without whom this book would still be a scattered assortment of photocopied pages in the bottom of a file drawer.

Our job as healthy parents
is to weave a safety net
beneath our children.

When we allow our children to become
caught in the midst of our adult conflicts,
used as pawns in our selfish games,
the safety net rips apart.
Our children are left insecure—
sad and angry and scared.

Our willingness
to put our conflicts aside,
to communicate constructively,
to provide consistency,
and to put their needs first, before our own,
weaves a tight net
which will catch them
every time they fall.

Contents

Preface

Keeping Kids Out of the Middle of What?

Set aside your logic and values for a moment, and enter the world of emotion.

This is the world in which intimate partnerships emerge between adults, sometimes in the span of a fleeting encounter, sometimes nurtured slowly over many months or years. A unique and often irrational mix of opportunity and necessity, hopes and expectations and beliefs, social pressures and physical appearances, hormones and body chemistry prompts two otherwise sensible human beings to create an intimate adult relationship.

Adult relationships need not be about sex. For some, physical intimacy is the first (and may remain the only) connection. For others, sexuality is gradually and slowly learned over time. For a silent minority, sexuality never plays a role. In this world of emotion, adult partnership is about mutual dependency—a "you and me against the world" kind of bond—with or without shared physical pleasure.

Adult partnerships are gender-blind. This book is not about politically correct, moral, and religious "how it is meant to be" values. This book is about the frank reality in which our children live. In this reality, it is often true that a man and a woman will become adult partners. It is also true that two men or two women can do the same.

Adult partnerships cross generations and ignore relatedness. In fact, partnerships among siblings and between parents and their adult children are the backbone of many trades and the centerpiece of many communities. Chances are good that there's something like a Smith and Son Lumber or a Jones Brothers Plumbing somewhere in your town. Long before these businesses arose, family members banded together to form partnerships within the home—mothers and daughters partnering as roommates, fathers and sons sharing the rent.

Adult partnership is not about marriage. Marriage is a social/legal institution that for centuries has sought to regulate and formalize adult partnerships. The simple fact is that adults can and always have formed committed bonds without formal governmental or religious endorsement.

And Without Marriage?

Without marriage, there can be no divorce. Intimate partnerships between adults begin and end every day all around us no matter the legal status, gender, generation, and sexual preferences or practices of the partners. Talking about the impact of divorce on children is like talking about the impact of global warming on the visible part of the iceberg. Both miss the larger reality.

In this world of emotion that you and I inhabit every day, a book about children's well-being must talk about the messy, entangled, politically incorrect, emotionally explosive reality that our children wake up to every morning and close their eyes upon every night. It is a reality that is often peppered with angry adult voices, slamming doors, bruised and broken bodies, sirens wailing, and caregivers who come and go unexpectedly. In this reality, the adult partners who together are supposed to weave a safety net beneath their children all too often selfishly draw their kids into their adult battles.

That's not me, you're thinking. *That's not my family.*

Perhaps not, but perhaps it is. The emotional pain that children suffer as a result of their parents' conflicts crosses every demographic, every state and every country, every religion and ethnicity. Families with multimillion-dollar annual incomes are as likely to expose their children to co-parental conflict as families living below the poverty line.

The problem is epidemic.

"But My Marriage Is Fine!"

That's terrific, but how's your co-parenting relationship?

Conventional, loving, happily married couples who would never intentionally put their children in the middle commonly do. Even in the best of adult relationships, poor communication, as well as subtly different beliefs and parenting practices, can leave the children caught in the middle.

Do you and your partner talk about parenting differences? Do you negotiate the new rules and expectations that must evolve as the kids grow? How do you update one another on the latest successes and struggles when you tag one another into the parenting ring?

Do you know what splitting and alienation are and how destructive they can be?

Read on. *Keeping Kids Out of the Middle* is as critically important to you in your happy, conventional marriage as it is to any other adult partners raising children.

Keeping Kids Out of the Middle is both a title and a mandate.

It is the mantra that we as parents must each repeat over and over and over to ourselves, recognizing that our responsibility to our children as parents and as co-parents goes on even when our intimate adult relationships crash and burn.

Co-Parents?

A very peculiar kind of math applies in the world of emotion. One adult plus one adult equals one role each. Call it what you will: hearthmate or lover, roommate or neighbor, significant other or spouse. As long as the relationship exists exclusively between two adults, each has a single role with regard to the other.

Once a child enters the formula—unexpected or long awaited, biologically or legally connected to one or both adults, infant or teen or in between—each adult suddenly has three roles: significant other to the adult partner, parent to the child, and co-parent with the child's other caregiver.

Among these three roles, only your intimate adult relationship—your role as hearthmate, lover, or spouse—can end. Many do. We know that more than 50 percent of all first marriages and nearly three out of four subsequent marriages end in divorce. Unfortunately, we have no way of knowing how many intimate adult partnerships never formalized by marriage end every day without the record-keeping benefit of becoming another hatch mark in the demographers' record books.

Your role as a parent cannot end. Left your child at daycare? You're still her parent. She's off to college? You're still her parent. She's grown and married and a parent herself? Yep, you're still her parent.

It's true that many biological parents give up their children for adoption. Whether this choice is made for financial or practical or health reasons, it can be the single most painful and selfless decision a human being can make. It is also true that, in some extreme instances, the legal system can relieve an adult of the privileges and responsibilities associated with parenthood. This is known as "termination of parental rights" (TPR). Whether formal, painful, or permanent, in the world of emotion neither giving up a child nor TPR can ever truly end a parent's role; once a parent, always a parent. Decades after the child is gone, a powerful sense of connection to another human being lingers.

And Your Role as a Co-Parent Is?

Once you're a co-parent, you are always a co-parent.

Like parenthood, your responsibility to your children's other caregiver for your kids' well-being must never end. It exists independent of your intimate adult relationship, surviving separation and divorce. No matter your feelings for your children's other parent, no matter the legal status of your adult partnership or of your role as parent, no matter the time or distance between you, you will always hold one end of the emotional safety net that defines your children's emotional security. Over time, others may enter the picture to help hold that net—a divorced parent's new partner, the teenage child's peers, or the young adult–child's own significant other—but your hand is always in there. Your strength is always needed. Your mature ability and willingness to hold it up will always matter.

When Feelings and Legalities Collide

The world of emotion and the legal world are often at odds, creating very real and very painful conflicts for parents and children alike.

In the world of emotions, your role as a parent and co-parent can never end. Your emotional connection to your child and your responsibility to his other parent supersedes all else. Your child's emotional connection to you and his experience of the mutual support or discord among his caregivers exists independent of any court order or edict.

Things are much more black-and-white in the legal world. Restraining orders and divorce decrees can create immediate and permanent barriers between co-parents or between parents and their children. The intense emotions built into these relationships go on undeterred even after the court has artificially severed the means to act upon them. Termination of parental rights and exclusive assignment of legal decision-making authority ("legal custody" in some states) or of residential responsibility ("physical custody" in some states) can put the world of emotion and legal reality at odds.

In each of these and in any similar circumstance, the law must always govern our behavior. What remains after every reasonable legal avenue has been exhausted for the disenfranchised adult (and perhaps for the child as well) is the painful process of grieving what has been lost and the hope of a distant reconnection.

Keeping Kids Out of the Middle is about co-parenting, the ancient art of cooperative caregiving. It's about recognizing and reconciling and prioritizing your three simultaneous roles as adult partner, parent, and co-parent. *Keeping Kids Out of the Middle* is about remaining a healthy parent and a child-centered co-parent no matter the state of your intimate adult relationship.

Are Your Kids Caught in the Middle?

Are your kids spectators on the sidelines of an adult war? Are they forced to listen or watch as the two people whom they love the most, the two people who together define their fragile sense of security and well-being, damn each other aloud?

Do your kids disappear when the adult tension gets so thick that you could cut it with a knife? Or do they scream and rant and cry for you to stop? Do they push their way between you and your co-parent, trying to mediate your differences, or do they carry the burden of the adult war with them to school, compromising their grades, their friendships, and their well-being?

Have your kids become messengers between you and their other parent within the same home or between separate homes? Are they forced to give up some part of their childhood because you and your co-parent cannot communicate? Must they carry sealed envelopes full of hatred or spoken messages full of deceit or—worse—are they made to keep secrets between you and their other parent?

Do they fear that loving one parent is a betrayal of the other?

Or are you pretending that they don't know, that they aren't affected, that they don't feel the constant, deep-sea pressure of living in a war zone? Are you rationalizing that the kids are too young to understand or too preoccupied with the latest video game to get it? How many times have you comforted yourself by saying, "They couldn't have overheard that argument. They were fast asleep upstairs!"

Wrong.

The kids know. They get it. Your kids breathe the emotional currents in your home. Your infant feels the tension in how you hold her. She hears the abrasive tone of your voice long before she understands the words. Your grade-schooler has his antennae up all of the time. The fact that he doesn't respond when you call him for lunch does not mean that he doesn't hear the argument in the kitchen. He does hear it, and your anger and sarcasm, hopelessness and fear become fault lines in the foundation of his self.

Do you think that they're asleep upstairs? Remember how you used to lie in bed, still and unmoving, with your eyes closed to fool your parents into thinking that you were asleep? If you had a penny for every child who listened at an air duct, who intercepted an e-mail, who snuck to the top of the stairs, who went through a parent's drawers, and who eavesdropped on the phone extension in the other room while Mom and Dad were fighting, you would be rich.

The kids know. They get it. They're watching and listening, which means that they are being caught in the middle.

Could it be that your kids' social withdrawal, declining grades, moodiness, anger, worry, or even their physical pain is due at least in part to their experience of adult conflict in their lives? Could the inattention that the teachers have started to notice really be due to the family upset rather than to a neurological problem that needs to be medicated?

Would you know it if your kids were being adultified or parentified or infantilized or alienated as a result of their experience of co-parental conflict? Have your children become chameleons in order to cope with differences between you and their other parent?

Keeping Kids Out of the Middle is about understanding all of these things. It's about working together to weave the best safety net possible underneath your kids no matter the state of your intimate adult relationship. It's about discovering how to be a healthy co-parent and raising healthier children in the process.

More Than Just Divorce

It is not news that divorce is epidemic in our country. One out of every two first marriages end in divorce, as do three out of every four second marriages. Every year, more than 1 million children in the United States experience a parent's divorce. In many communities, children who live in intact biological families are the exception, rather than the rule.

Divorce doesn't need to harm children.

If you set aside all of the provocative moral and ethical and religious and political controversy, the simple psychological fact is that divorce need have no more impact on your kids than registering your car or filing a tax return. Divorce is, after all, just a legal landmark along an already emotionally supercharged path. It need be nothing more than the collection of official documents and bureaucratic acknowledgments of something that exists and hurts long before and may continue long after the papers are signed and notarized and filed away.

To say that a child's problem is his parents' divorce is like saying that the patient's problem is his rash. Each is a visible, countable (How many kids experience divorce? How many patients have rashes?), public symptom of a larger problem that existed long before it was evident and is likely to persist long after. The patient has Lyme disease, an auto-immune illness that is often recognized because of its characteristic bull's-eye-like rash. The child is a victim of co-parental conflict, an insidious pathology that may have existed his whole life but only became evident when the divorce appeared.

The Costs of Divorce

Divorce doesn't need to harm children, but it often does. This happens for at least two reasons.

First, the vast majority of divorce attorneys and the courts in which they practice approach the process with the same adversarial intent as they would any criminal matter. Someone must be found guilty, and someone must be found innocent. This process is built on antagonism and escalating acrimony. Molehills of difference are easily and often inflated into mountains of discord all in the interest of "winning." When co-parents allow themselves to become polarized by the zealous advocates they hire, the children's best interests are routinely compromised. Rather than approach the end of the intimate adult relationship from the healthy perspective of assuring the children's continued well-being, adversarial attorneys and courts promote an adult-centered, win/lose mentality.

The alternative, known as "collaborative law," is discussed in Chapter 11.

The second way in which divorce can and does often harm children is financial. The divorce process can be astronomically expensive, particularly when the children's custody is disputed. It is not at all uncommon for parents to deplete savings accounts, to spend inheritances, and to compromise their children's college funds all in the interest of winning another hour or two each week of a child's time. This, together with gender inequities in the contemporary U.S. legal system and in employee compensation, means that the average annual postdivorce income for a custodial mother's household drops even while the father's finances may *improve*. The result is a very real cost in terms of the children's future opportunities.

And so it is with divorce: the pain exists regardless of the paperwork. Our children endure our selfish, adult upsets with more or less anger and fear and sadness regardless of whether the relationship was ever notarized by the state or dissolved by a judge. Our responsibility to our kids as their parents and to one another as co-parents is not changed in the least by the legal status of our adult relationship.

Divorce doesn't need to harm our children, but co-parental conflict routinely does.

Why? Think about cars. People, like cars, need to be refueled. In healthy families, children are refueled by their parents. Parents are refueled by one another. When the intimate adult relationship fails, each parent's gas tank runs low. Each parent has less to give the kids, and the kids suffer for it.

The toddler seated on Mom's lap in an unfamiliar room, for example, scans the environment curiously only for so long. Once she feels safe, she clambers down to the floor and toddles off. When she becomes tired or scared or hungry or hurt, she calls for comfort. Her tank is empty. She calls to Mom to be refueled the same way that you might call AAA if you're stranded by the side of the road.

If Mom's tank is full, she responds calmly. She reassures with a loving word or a pick-up, a kiss or a cuddle. If Mom's own gas tank is empty because she's embroiled in adult turmoil (or otherwise stressed), she will predictably be less sensitive and responsive to her child's needs. She might respond to her toddler's call for help abruptly with irritation or reluctantly with despair. Either way, the child receives less comfort and reassurance—less emotional fuel—and grows anxious and clingy or angry and resentful.

This is just one of the relatively benign and all too common ways that a child can be caught in the middle.

Role Reversal?

When co-parental conflict leaves a parent emotionally drained, some parents turn to their children for comfort. This reversal may initially feel rewarding to the child ("Mommy needs me!"), but it is ultimately very destructive. This is the path to adultification, parentification, or infantilization. These unhealthy dynamics are described in Chapter 14.

Co-parental conflict has a second, more practical, and measurable impact on kids.

Conflict interferes with communication. Angry people share less. What they do share, they share less effectively. Details are left out. Nuances are ignored. A stressed adult relationship leaves each parent reluctant to speculate or guess or wonder out loud about "what if's" and "what could be's." These more relaxed communications often help people to think more creatively and to anticipate a broader range of possibilities. When communication becomes rigid and terse, the adult caregiving team becomes less effective. Details fall through the cracks. Opportunities are missed. Situations arise that aren't anticipated. Flexibility is diminished. As a result, the kids grow more and more disappointed and angry. Their upset further stresses the co-parents, whose communications fail even further. The holes in the safety net that the co-parents should be holding grow bigger and bigger until the child inevitably falls through or dives through. The school-aged child who recognizes the gaps in her parents' consistency and the failure of their communication can take advantage of the situation. She can drive a wedge in the middle, winning herself undeserved and inappropriate opportunities even while her sense of emotional security is shaken. This action is called "splitting" (see Chapter 13).

Each of these concerns—impaired emotional refueling, infantilization, adultification, parentification, alienation, or splitting—is discussed in detail in the pages that follow. But none of these are caused by divorce. These and similarly destructive dynamics arise when co-parents conflict, when communication and consistency fail, and when children are caught in the middle.

What This Book Is and
What This Book Is Not

Keeping *Kids Out of the Middle* is about giving your kids an emotional foundation upon which they can build a healthy self and strong relationships, no matter the legal status, physical distance, or emotional ties between you and your caregiving partner. It's about collaborating with your co-parent to weave a safety net underneath your children to catch them when they fall and to give them the security of knowing that it's always there, even when they don't need it.

Keeping Kids Out of the Middle is an exercise in maturity. It will help you and your co-parent develop impulse control and empathy, as well as the perspective-taking skills and the practical strategies necessary to put your children's needs first, before your own. It will help you to put aside your feelings about your adult partner so the kids whom you share will be healthier.

This book is not a recipe for self-sacrifice or martyrdom. Raising healthy children and functioning as part of a successful co-parenting team does not mean ignoring or neglecting your own feelings and needs.

Keeping Kids Out of the Middle will help you develop the means and establish the resources necessary to make sure that your emotional gas tank remains full and available to refuel your kids. The concept of "keeping kids out of the middle" simply means separating your adult feelings and needs from the business of co-parenting.

"The business of co-parenting"? Yes, *Keeping Kids Out of the Middle* talks about co-parenting as a businesslike process. This book will help you and your co-parent establish a child-centered agenda, revising it as circumstances change and the kids grow, drawing up action plans, and collaborating and cooperating in accomplishing specific child-centered goals.

Keeping Kids Out of the Middle is a how-to book for co-parents:

- How to better understand and meet your children's needs.
- How to distinguish between your children's needs and your children's wants.
- How to distinguish between that which helps your children be healthy and that which makes them happy (and how to cope better with the inevitable choice between the two).
- How to keep your children's needs front and center, apart from your own.
- How to establish and improve consistency and communications with your co-parent(s).
- How to continue to meet your children's needs as your family changes.
- How to take the high road every time, even if you believe that your parenting partner does not.

What This Book Is Not

Keeping Kids Out of the Middle is the exercise program for those of us whose maturity muscles have been atrophied in a world ever more full of immediate gratification and me-me-me now-now-now. It is the recipe book for those of us who believe that we know what we're doing as parents but fear that our parenting partners may not. This book is the first instruction manual to recognize that the critical basics of co-parenting must be learned long before and quite apart from any discussion of marriage or divorce.

Be aware that reading *Keeping Kids Out of the Middle* cannot solve your problems. It will not save your troubled adult relationship, it cannot magically change your difficult co-parent, and it cannot raise your children for you. Like any exercise program or recipe book or instruction manual, *Keeping Kids Out of the Middle* can only offer you new ways of thinking and new strategies for behaving. It is ultimately up to you and your co-parent to make them work.

Keeping Kids Out of the Middle is not about morals, ethics, religion, or politics. It is not pro- or anti-divorce; pro- or anti-cohabitation; pro– or anti–gay marriage, -domestic partnering, -grandparents' rights, -foster or adoptive parenting. It is simply and insistently over and over again pro-child and pro-health. The simple, clear message is contained in the title: *Keeping Kids Out of the Middle.*

This book does not provide legal advice. Although many matters of law arise in the context of learning to better understand and collaboratively respond to your kids' needs, you should not mistake this book as a substitute for the expert advice of a trusted family law attorney.

Because laws vary by state and are constantly evolving, *Keeping Kids Out of the Middle* is no more than a stepping-stone for all legal and court-related matters.

Neither does this book provide medical advice. Impaired co-parenting, family conflict, separation, and divorce can be associated with stress, which in turn can cause physical symptoms often mistaken for everything from ulcer to migraine, from reflux to insomnia. Some unknown percentage of children diagnosed, treated, and/or medicated for depression, anxiety, bipolar disorder, oppositional-defiant disorder, and attention deficit disorder (ADD/ADHD) should more accurately be considered the victims of their family turmoil. When any such physical, psychiatric, or psychological symptoms arise, this book must never take the place of firsthand consultation with trusted medical and mental health experts.

Finally, *Keeping Kids Out of the Middle* is not a parenting primer. Parenting has to do with the one-on-one relationship between an adult caregiver and a child. Every library and bookstore has scores of excellent parenting books, some of which are listed in the resources at the back of this book. Although many of the ideas and strategies discussed here may be helpful to parenting, *Keeping Kids Out of the Middle* is about co-parenting: the collaborative, child-centered relationship between two (or more) adults who share an interest in a child's well-being.

Of course, *Keeping Kids Out of the Middle* is not about you. It is written about millions of people who may be like you and your co-parents and your kids in many ways, but no book can ever adequately account for the particular constellation of strengths and weaknesses, hopes and fears, history and circumstances that make your own and your kids' situation unique. You must read with one eye open to the unique realities that frame your world, adapting these words to the specifics of your experience.

As a child-centered clinician, I wear many hats, each of which puts me on the front lines of co-parenting battles—providing therapy to children from happy, healthy, and intact families and from those in which the co-parents despise one another; sitting between adults who have nothing in common but their love for a child; working directly with separated or divorced parents in an effort to improve their co-parenting skills because their child is hurting; serving the court as a guardian ad litem, as an expert witness, or while conducting a family systems (custody) evaluation. In each of these distinct professional roles, I have observed that one simple fact remains true: **co-parents who can agree to put their children's needs before their own raise healthier children.**

This single observation is the foundation upon which this book rests.

Keeping your kids out of the middle is a goal I would have you work toward every day, no matter how old your child, how challenging the circumstance, how beloved or despised your parenting partner. It is, in fact, the single most important goal that guides me as a professional and as a husband and a father.

I must add this: I am not fond of labels and diagnoses.

Unfortunately, because psychology is the stepchild of medicine, mental health practice across disciplines in the United States is often focused on identifying and categorizing an individual's pathology. If you bring your concerns about your child's fears, worries, sadness, anger, or relationships to a mental health professional, most will respond the same way that a pediatrician thinks about a child's tummy ache. They will label the problem with a diagnosis and prescribe a treatment. The common bias is to look for causes inside the child. That approach works well in a medical context if the cause is a ruptured appendix or a broken bone, but fails miserably when the child's distress is a symptom of something outside of his body, like family dysfunction. As a clinician, I maintain that it is at least as important to look at how the child is responding to the world in which he lives—the family system—as it is to listen to how the world in which he lives is responding to him.

This is the approach that I have taken in writing *Keeping Kids Out of the Middle*. Our goal together in the pages that follow is to understand how the family system impacts the child and, by improving co-parenting, to improve the health and well-being of our kids.

A Word About Words

This book and the work that informs it are unbiased with regard to race, gender, culture, sexual orientation, religion, politics, age, generation, and a host of other factors that combine to define how your child's circumstance is unique from all others.

Unfortunately, our language is quite limited. In the interest of political correctness and in a genuine effort to address the full range of readers' experiences, writers constantly face the awkward mandate of "his/her" and "s/he." Not only would unprejudiced reference to every combination of gender, generation, legal status, and such make this book very long, it would make most sentences too dense to understand.

Thus, in the interest of readability and with advance apologies for any misunderstandings, the chapters that follow are simplified in very specific ways:

1. "He" and "she" are used arbitrarily to refer to a given parent's choices or a given child's behavior. Unless otherwise specified, the sentences "Your son puts on his shoes" and "Your co-parent may say that her phone is broken" are simplifications of expression with no specific gender implications.

2. "Parent" and "caregiver" are used interchangeably to refer to any adult who has responsibility for the well-being of any child. In its narrowest meaning, this refers to the adults in the child's home or homes. In its broadest meaning, a child's caregivers include teachers, daycare providers, babysitters, coaches, tutors, and such. Differences among caregivers as co-parents are discussed in Chapter 2.

3. "Mom" or "mother" and "dad" or "father" are two kinds or caregivers among many. These terms are used interchangeably as familiar references without bias for gender or legal, biological, or genetic relationships. No distinction is made in these pages between caregivers who give birth to their own genetic offspring, those who give birth to others' genetic contributions via assisted reproductive technologies, and those who adopt, enter as stepparents, or provide foster care, although each variation on the general theme of parenthood carries with it its own unique challenges.

4. "Child" and "children," "kid(s)," and "son" and "daughter" are used

interchangeably without deference to gender or number. It's just too darn awkward to read "child(ren)" and "son/daughter" all the time.

5. "Intimate adult partner" is any adult who helps to refuel you emotionally. This phrase is used throughout this book to refer to that adult with whom you share (or perhaps once shared but no longer share) an intense, positive emotional bond. This person might be (or at least once was) your significant other, domestic partner, hearthmate, husband, or wife, but might equally well be a roommate, sibling, or one of your own parents. The intimacy you share (or once shared) is emotional without any implication of a sexual or physical relationship.

6. By contrast, a "co-parent" or "parenting partner" is any adult with whom you share a responsibility to a child. Although your intimate partner might also be your co-parent (and vice versa), this is not always the case. Whether or not you share this book with your intimate adult partner, please do share it with your co-parent. *Keeping Kids Out of the Middle* is written for both of you.

7. The phrase "parent-on-duty" or "POD" is used often throughout this book. The POD is the caregiver who is there on the front line with the kids. When parenting partners live together, the POD might simply be the parent who happens to be in the backyard or the kitchen when a problem arises. When co-parents live apart, the POD is the caregiver who has residential responsibility (formerly known as "physical custody") for the kids. By contrast, the POD's co-parent is sometimes referred to as the "absent parent," describing nothing more than that caregiver's distance from the action at the time that it occurred.

8. When children migrate between their parents' separate homes (as when divorced parents share residential responsibility for their kids), the "sending parent" is distinguished from the "receiving parent" largely to discuss the transition between the homes. The sending parent is the caregiver who is relinquishing residential responsibility (the outgoing POD). The receiving parent is the caregiver who is stepping into the role of POD and accepting residential responsibility for the kids.

Finally, a word about metaphor: over time, psychology has invented its own arcane vocabulary with which to describe the interrelated processes of child development, parenting, and co-parenting. Rather than ask you to wade through unnecessary, polysyllabic, and hyperbolic descriptions of individuation, introjection, and superego lacunae (as examples), I've taken the liberty of presenting the most relevant and useful among these concepts in the language of metaphor.

In particular, co-parents are described throughout this book as "weaving a safety net," which instills security, and as "laying a foundation" upon which a child might build a strong and stable self. Together, these two rather dissimilar images serve to illustrate what healthy parents have known for centuries and science only has recently come around to validating: just as every human being receives twenty-three chromosomes from each of his genetic progenitors (who are sometimes also his parents), we each also receive a psychological piece of each of our primary caregivers throughout the course of growing up. When these separate pieces are mutually compatible, we have a good chance of growing up healthy and well. When these pieces are incompatible—too disparate or conflicted—we may find ourselves vulnerable and in pain.

Take Care Not to Be a Squeaky-Wheel Caregiver!

It's easy to become consumed by the practical necessities that surround us—bills, laundry, work, and house cleaning, to name just a few—and distracted by the conflict in an intimate adult relationship. When this means that you're too preoccupied and upset to pay attention to your kids' successes ("Look, Mommy!") but are forced to pay attention to their upsets ("She hurt me!"), you've become a squeaky-wheel parent.

A parent who only pays attention to a child's misbehavior will discover that the child's misbehavior becomes more frequent and more severe. Why not? That child craves your attention and affection. When the only reliable way of getting this critical emotional fuel is by misbehaving, he'll misbehave more and more often.

As healthy parents, we must learn to put aside our stresses, to compartmentalize our adult conflicts, and to remain present and available to catch our kids succeeding. When compliance and success wins our affection and attention, our kids can learn to succeed.

We must never allow ourselves to only oil the wheel that squeaks.

A Daily Communication Exercise

Improving co-parenting communication in the interest of improving consistency is a constant and critical process. This simple exercise can help:

Make the time every day to relate one parenting incident to your co-parent. Tell a story about a challenge that came up that day. "When Billy asked me for a cookie today, here's what I did . . ." or "Rachel hit her brother, so I . . ." End the story with, "What would you have done?" Your routine effort to discuss small incidents will improve your consistency and your communication skills so that co-parenting crises arise less often, and, when they do, you and your parenting partner will be better prepared to cope with them.

The need for consistency is just as important for a married mom and dad who alternate bedtime responsibilities in a single home; for the never married, separated, or divorced mom and dad whose children migrate between their homes; and for the mother and adult son who share responsibilities for his twin daughters in different homes. And later, if and when a new parenting partner enters the picture, consistency will help everyone adjust to the new and expanded family.

Structure Decreases Everyone's Anxiety

Psychology acknowledges far too few universal truths, but here are three of them:

- Anxiety interferes with mature functioning and fuels conflict.
- Structure decreases anxiety.
- Human beings resist structure, especially when it is first introduced. This is called "limit testing."

Because co-parental conflict sparks anxiety in parenting partners as well as in kids, our goal must be to decrease anxiety. We do this in part by increasing structure, confident that structure will benefit everyone involved and knowing that our kids will inevitably test the structures that we provide.

Consider speed limits as an analogy: Speed limits reassure most adults (although there are always a few who think that it would be fun to have no speed limits!), but few drivers actually abide by them until ticketed. We test the very structures that reassure us.

Parenting structure comes in four basic forms:

1. *Structure means limits and consequences associated with specific behaviors.* A limit defines what behavior is acceptable and what behavior is not acceptable. When limits are clear and known in advance, kids know how to succeed and have a better chance of doing so. When limits shift with Dad's mood or with Mom's drinking, or are otherwise random and chaotic, success becomes

impossible. The result is escalating anxiety, anger, and depression.

Unfortunately, the term "consequences" has taken on a negative meaning as if it were synonymous with "punishment." In fact, a consequence is simply a predictable outcome associated with a given action or inaction. A consequence is the second domino that falls when the first is knocked over. It's the result in the formula, *If A, then B*. Whenever possible, healthy parents strive to catch their children succeeding so that positive consequences (rewards) can be provided.

When consequences are expectable and valued, positive outcomes become incentives, consequences that motivate acceptable and desirable behaviors. When expectable consequences are negative and meaningful, they become disincentives, motivating children to avoid undesirable behaviors.

2. *Structure means consistency across environments.* When caregivers establish and maintain similar parenting expectations and consequences, children become less anxious. The flip side of that coin is true as well: when caregivers have very different expectations and consequences, children become more anxious. Conflicts erupt, punctuated by angry or whining complaints that sound like, "But Mom lets us . . ." and "When Dad's here we can . . . !"

In the extreme, children experience the transition between very different caregivers as a kind of culture shock. Adjusting to transitions between different caregiving styles in a single home or between very different homes exhausts and frustrates them, interfering with learning, playing, and growing.

Of course, there are a million details of parenting that may be more or less consistent between caregivers, some large and obvious (bedtime, curfew, homework, for example) and others that are smaller but may be no less important (media restrictions, privacy rules, bathroom behavior, for example). Because kids grow and circumstances change, parenting expectations and consequences are always changing; consistency between caregivers thus requires constant communication.

3. *Structure means predictability over time.* When kids know what to expect, anxiety diminishes. Parenting expectations and consequences—and for that matter, each parent's mood and behavior—should be predictable from one day to the next. Kids who find their caregivers' behavior unpredictable or even random are at very high risk for serious emotional disturbance and relationship difficulties later in life.

   Predictability can be enhanced by establishing routines and rituals. A routine is simply an A-B-C sequence that is expected over and over again. Getting ready for bed, as one example, can be a challenge for many young children. Bedtime can be, after all, a scary experience of separation and loss associated with the dark at the time of day when most people are psychologically weakest and most vulnerable. One way to improve bedtime compliance and decrease associated anxiety is by creating a pre-bed routine—for example, bath-story-cuddle-sleep. Similar routines can be established to help with after-school organization (snack-play-homework-supper) and wake-up (bathroom-dress-breakfast-bus).

   A ritual is a routine imbued with special (magical) meaning. For example, many young kids struggle when they first transition from one home to another. Emotions associated with separation from the sending parent, among other causes, can fuel anxiety and upset. Some of this can be combated by creating an arrival ritual in the receiving parent's home. At every transition, Mom and the kids sit on the floor in a circle and sing the "Mom's House" song (to the tune of your favorite nursery rhyme):

Here we are at mom's house, mom's house, mom's house;

Here we are at mom's house, and I know what we do.

At mom's house we use nice words . . .

4. *Structure means boundaries that define space.* Boundaries define physical space and territory. They can be real, visible, tangible boundaries like baby gates and bathroom doors, or psychological boundaries that define personal space. Boundaries help to distinguish what is mine from what is yours. Boundaries between homes help to define family, while boundaries within homes help to define individuality.

Because growing up from infancy onward is a process of defining "me" versus "not-me" (often referred to as "individuation"), the need for boundaries within homes changes over time. Infants often share space with parents. Toddlers move back and forth from parents to a separate space of their own. Grade-schoolers can become very territorial and creative about defining their possessions and their space, all in preparation for the self-conscious, very private preferences of high-schoolers.

Defining boundaries can be particularly important when

co-parents live apart. Children often have an easier time migrating between two homes when they have a space defined in each house that is uniquely their own. This might be as elaborate as a bedroom, as simple as a drawer or a shelf, or just a box that the child has decorated and declared his own with a sign that says, "Stay Out!"

Boundaries are also important when co-parents separate because they help to define "family." It is often useful to explain, "Once upon a time we all lived together and made one family. Now that we live apart." The parent explains to the children, "You have two families: one in this house, another at the other house."

Keeping Kids Out of the Middle will help you understand what children need, what they go through, and how to create a safety net for them by setting limits, drawing boundaries, and creating routines. Communication, consistency, and the wisdom to know here and now, in the calm between the storms, that the kids' needs must always come first—these are the ingredients that we have to work with. What follows is the recipe handed down over generations but too often lost in the crush and hustle of the modern world. It is the recipe for raising healthy children, the formula for keeping kids out of the middle.

Chapter 1

What Is a Co-Parent?

W e've heard frequently over the last few decades that "it takes a village to raise a child."

It is true that one parent alone might be able to manage a child's behavior. One parent alone might be able to provide a child with food, clothing, and shelter, to serve as an emotional anchor, a role model, a mentor, and a support. One parent alone might be able to give her child all the necessary building blocks of good health and future happiness—except one.

One parent raising a child alone cannot give a child a model of healthy collaboration, mutual respect, and shared intimacy. Certainly these things exist between parent and child, but it's not the same. When adults work together to raise a child, the child has the opportunity to learn about reciprocity and teamwork, about communication and compromise.

Raising healthy children is about far more than good nutrition and annual checkups, toilet training, and soccer practice; mastering A-B-C,

1-2-3, and the SAT. Raising healthy children is about more than providing the emotional anchor that allows a child to go out in the world to
explore, feeling safe, secure, and trusted. These developmental steps
are necessary, but are hardly sufficient.

Raising healthy children is also about helping our kids discover how
to navigate intimate relationships.

The conventional wisdom that we each learn how to develop our
later intimate relationships from our early parent/child interactions is
like claiming that we can learn to ride a bicycle while the training
wheels are still on. Managing the parent/child relationship may be each
child's first step toward creating healthy intimate adult relationships,
but it's not enough. It's artificial. It's a rigged game in which the child
always wins.

A healthy parent/child relationship is a one-way street in which the
parent gives and the child takes. A child's experience of caregiving lays
the foundation for the later experience of nurturance: how to give and
how to get caring from others.

A healthy intimate adult relationship is a two-way street. It's about
complementary needs, emotions, and feelings, and it's defined by a
give-and-take reciprocity that should not exist between parent and
child—and, if it did, would be unhealthy. The child who is launched into
adulthood without any experience outside of the parent/child relationship is in for a surprise.

The child's experience of the co-parenting relationship creates the
foundation upon which he begins to build a sense of intimacy and
reciprocity, from first friendships in grade school to first crushes in junior high and onward, to shape his intimate adult partnerships. As

co-parents, you are doing much more than spelling one another when you're overwhelmed, tired, or sick. You are actively modeling how peers communicate and respect one another. You are implicitly teaching your kids how to compromise and negotiate, express feelings, and support one another.

Raising a healthy child is a team sport. It requires the active contribution and collaboration of two or more adults who share a critical interest in that child's well-being. These collaborators bring a breadth of skills and interests, resources and experiences, needs and hopes and fears to the process. How these sometimes complementary, sometimes contradictory puzzle pieces come together is what co-parenting is about.

How to manage this collaboration is the subject of this book.

A co-parent is a teammate, one among two or more adults who share a goal. A co-parent is by choice, mandate, or happenstance a member of the team that is responsible for the well-being of one or more children. As is the case with any team, success or failure depends largely on the cooperation, communication, and coordination of its members. It depends on each member's ability to see that his own needs are met elsewhere, that he comes to the team activity refreshed, refueled, and ready to give. The team's success depends upon each member's willingness and ability to put aside their own ego needs—to tag-team and pinch-hit, even to sacrifice—in favor of the needs of the group as a whole.

Think about co-parenting like your favorite team sport, anything from soccer to synchronized swimming to bobsledding. Even NASCAR racing, featuring individual drivers and their vehicles, depends largely on the split-second collaboration and constant communication between the driver and the members of his pit crew. Co-parenting works precisely the same way: one adult may be driving at any given time—the parent-on-duty (POD)—but the co-parenting team's success depends on the close cooperation, focused communication, and consistent support of each member of the parenting team.

A successful car racing team wins the checkered flag and prize money and the opportunity to win more races. A successful co-parenting team wins the mutual pride and pleasure of sending a healthy child off into the world to create her own healthy adult relationships.

A co-parenting team often includes one or both of a child's birth parents, but may not. In some instances, one or both of the birth parents are absent or deceased, unwilling, or legally prohibited from participating. Co-parents commonly include one or both of a child's birth parents' chosen intimate adult partners (called stepparents when the relationship is formalized by marriage), others among a child's biological relatives (grandparents, aunts, uncles, for example), chosen or hired caregivers (nannies, babysitters, tutors, for example), and even special friends and neighbors.

A co-parent can be any size, shape, or color and can have any religious belief, sexual orientation or practice, political affiliation, gender identity, or shoe size. Co-parents can live together under one roof or on different continents. Co-parents may be one another's intimate adult partners (as is the conventional case in an intact, nuclear family) or may despise one another (as is tragically the case among a small percentage of separated and divorced co-parents).

Who Participates on the Co-Parenting Team?

Start by assuming that all the adults who participate in caring for a child should be actively invited to contribute to the co-parenting team.

This situation is easiest among co-parents who have chosen one another, as when a couple marries and has children. In this most conventional of arrangements, Mom and Dad each wear three different hats: they are one another's intimate partner (spouse), they are parents to their children, and they are each other's co-parent.

Things become more complicated as the kids get older, and their social worlds expand beyond the home and the backyard. Babysitters and nannies, teachers and coaches, religious leaders, and counselors and tutors play a more or less important role on the co-parenting team.

The question of who plays on the co-parenting team is broadened even further when assisted reproductive technologies (sperm or egg donation, surrogate gestational mothers) and the law (foster placement or adoption, termination of parental rights) introduce or restrict still other real or potential players to the co-parenting team. Even when these could-be parents never actually materialize, they can become very real and powerful psychological forces in the minds of the children who learn about their existence. We all know stories, for example, about the teenager adopted at birth who runs away from home to discover his "real" parents.

And then there are the X-games of co-parenting—the extreme tests of cooperative caregiving, those circumstances that can challenge the most mature, child-centered parents among us: when Mom and Dad separate (with or without divorce), for example, and one or both adults introduce a new intimate partner into the equation. Suddenly, a caregiver can find herself forced to collaborate with a person whom she's never before met, whom she may not like but who is undeniably (and perhaps even unexpectedly) a part of the child's world and thereby her new co-parent.

Unresolved grief over the failed relationship, unfamiliarity and distrust, resentment and competitiveness, territoriality over the child's origins, practices and beliefs that may have contributed to or even caused the original couple to split and which have since been amplified by court-induced antagonism or divergent life choices—these are among the extreme emotional hurdles that can feel like Mount Everests to be climbed.

Television gives us common points of reference with which to illustrate these various co-parenting constellations:

In the good old, idealized *Leave It to Beaver* days of yore, growing up with Mom and Dad was the norm. Ward and June Cleaver each had the other as co-parents. Period. Family was defined narrowly within the terms of (a very chauvinistic) marriage and the shared walls of a single home. White picket fence—you know the image.

A decade later, *The Brady Bunch* began to open our eyes to the idea of the blended family. Mike Brady and Carol married and combined their respective broods to create a new family group of eight: two widowed parents plus his three boys and her three girls. Reading between the lines of the program's syrupy scripts, Marsha's teenage upsets over her complexion and preteen Bobby's athletic failings and older brother Greg's first crush were all exercises in collaborative caregiving: Should

Carol tell husband Mike that her daughter Cindy got in trouble at school? Can Mike make a decision about Peter's haircut without first checking with stepmother Carol? Will the boys get away with telling their stepmom one thing and their father another? Or will Mike and Carol compare notes and discover how those mischievous boys tried to split (drive a wedge between) them? And never adequately resolved, but often at issue, was where the well-meaning homemaker/nanny/comic foil Alice fit in. Should she have been involved as a co-parent? Was she allied with the kids?

From our twenty-first-century perspective, these *Brady Bunch* questions seem tame, even laughable. Our concept of family has become so broad and diffuse that the Bradys' dilemmas barely even grab our attention. Today's media doesn't hesitate to introduce us to children being raised jointly by unrelated, same-sex caregivers (*Full House*), by intergenerational co-parents (*Judging Amy*), by extended families (*Everybody Loves Raymond*), and by parents raising children largely on their own (*Gilmore Girls*). Curiously, although homosexuality is far from forbidden (*Will and Grace*), at this writing there is not yet a mainstream sitcom or drama featuring gay or lesbian co-parents.

In the world that surrounds us, co-parenting must indeed be considered very broadly. It is seldom obvious which adults should or actually do work together in the best interests of any particular child. What stands out all too readily are the children whose caregivers are at odds, pulling the child painfully into the midst of their selfish conflicts.

Chapter 2

Not All Co-Parents
Are Created Equal

Back in the *Leave It to Beaver* days, the division of labor among co-parents was simple and clear. In the role of husband and father, the male served as breadwinner, decision maker, and ultimate authority. His partner, in the role of subservient wife and mother to his children, was a full-time homemaker, house cleaner, diaper changer, and cook. She handled the moment-to-moment parenting issues, deferring the more substantial and recalcitrant child-rearing and behavior-management challenges to the father/husband. To quote June Cleaver of *Leave It to Beaver* fame, for example, "Wait until your father gets home!" Such was the sexist, authoritarian chauvinism of the 1950s and early 1960s, a generation that was taught quite explicitly that "Father knows best."

The women's movement for social, political, and employment equality begun in the 1960s has created an unexpected backlash: with more women in the workforce, more fathers have devoted themselves to raising their children. As the chauvinism and stereotypes that characterized our parents' and their parents' generations have receded, parenting has become less and less gender-specific. Today, men and women can play equal roles as caregivers and as co-parents.

This is not to say that men and women play equal roles as co-parents in every instance. Important differences of parenting authority routinely do exist, but less and less often as a function of a parent's gender. Instead, these differences are more typically determined by personality, by context (the time and place an individual exercises his caregiving responsibilities), by mutual decision within the co-parenting team, and sometimes by the courts.

Differences Among Co-Parents Determined by the Law and the Courts

Although laws differ by region, the legal system has generally been reluctant to tell parents how to raise their children. There are a handful of clear exceptions to this principle, including laws regulating child labor, mandating education, and prohibiting abuse and neglect. The most common exception to this principle, however, are those laws and rulings that determine how a child's care is to be divided among her various potential caregivers.

In general, the law entrusts a child's married birth parents with mutual decision-making authority. Unfortunately, this overly simplistic rule is sufficient only for a shrinking minority of children. The growing number of unmarried mothers (who are sometimes minors themselves), high-tech reproductive technologies (that can involve separate egg and sperm donors, and surrogate gestational and birth mothers), the legalities of foster and adoptive parenting, issues associated with gay marriage and domestic partnering and civil unions, and the grandparents' rights movement (to name just a few) keep the courts very busy. Add to this the flood of divorces, custody actions, and paternity suits, and it quickly becomes clear that the exceptions outnumber the general rule by far.

As a place to begin, it is useful to understand the basic distinctions that often bear on determining parenting and co-parenting responsibilities.

A child's *guardian* is legally responsible for the child's care. The legal guardian has the authority to make decisions in the child's life (medical treatment, school enrollment, religious affiliations, for example) and is held responsible for the child's well-being, as when concerns about abuse or neglect arise.

Legal guardianship can be associated with a single adult, as when an unmarried woman gives birth or adopts and no father is recognized, or it can be shared by two (or more) adults, as when a father is identified on a birth or adoption certificate and shares responsibility for the child with the mother regardless of marital status. Less commonly, guardianship for a child can be assigned by a court to an agency (child protective services, for example) or to a court-designated proxy (a guardian ad litem, for example).

Guardianship can be legally terminated (TPR), as when an adult is determined to present a danger to a child, to be chronically absent from a child's life, or judged to be unable to adequately care for the child. When guardianship is unknown or is terminated, an agency or institution can be named as the child's guardian, as when a child becomes a ward of the court.

A child's _custodian_ (or _custodial parent_) can be the same person as her guardian, or may be different. A custodian is the individual or agency responsible for the child's day-to-day care. When, for example, the court becomes a child's legal guardian, a foster parent or institution may be assigned custodial responsibilities. In this instance, the custodial parent manages routine matters such as meals, homework, and bedtime, but must defer to the guardian (the court) when larger questions arise, such as changing the child's name or having elective surgery.

Who Are the Co-Parents?

Mark and Mary are married and living together. They have a five-year-old son named Max. Mark and Mary happily share guardianship (legal decision-making authority) and custodial (day-to-day care) responsibilities for their little boy.

John and Joanne live together with their four-year-old son, Jason. Although they're not married, they also share guardianship and custodial responsibilities for their child.

Few people are aware that Mark and Joanne were once married. They had a son named Junior who is now fifteen years old. Junior lives full-time with his mother (Joanne) and her partner (John), visiting with his father (Mark) and stepmother (Mary) infrequently. At the time of Mark and Joanne's divorce (when Junior was just two years old), the court granted them shared legal decision-making authority. Mark and Joanne must thus continue working together to make decisions for Junior.

Junior wants to attend a private high school. Can Joanne make this decision alone?

No, probably not (although she would be wise to consult with an attorney to be perfectly clear). Because she and Mark share decision-making authority, she has an obligation to discuss the matter with him first.

Should Joanne consult with her live-in partner, John, in considering this decision?

Legally, she may not have to. Even though John lives in the same home, has helped Junior with his homework since kindergarten, and raised him like his own son, he has no legal authority to make decisions in Junior's life.

What about psychologically? Mark may resent John's involvement, but Junior needs to know that John is involved.

How should Joanne respond to Junior's pestering questions: "So Mom, can I go to Local Prep next year or not?"

What happens when Joanne suggests that her younger son, Jason, should transfer to the private elementary school affiliated with Local Prep? Joanne should certainly discuss this question with her co-parent (Jason's father), John, but should she talk to Mark about it? To Mary? Neither has any legal responsibility to Jason (and Mary has never met the child). Nevertheless, the sibling relationship between Junior and Max will be impacted by this decision, as will the finances available to fund the kids' tuitions. As a respectful and child-centered co-parent, Joanne should at least alert Mark and Mary that she'd like both kids to be enrolled. And at best? Perhaps Mark, Mary, John, and Joanne can all work together to determine where their combined brood should go to school and how best to pay for it.

Three Questions the Court Will Ask

When co-parents seek a legal separation or divorce, the court must address at least three questions:

1. *Should the intimate adult relationship be terminated?* With few exceptions, one party's wish is sufficient for the court to grant a legal separation or divorce.

2. *How should legal decision-making authority (guardianship) for the child be allotted upon termination of the intimate adult relationship?* The court's presumption is usually that the co-parents will continue to share legal decision-making authority and work together to serve the child's best interests despite their adult differences. In some cases, however, one parent will be granted legal decision-making authority in a specific area of the child's life (medical or educational decisions, for example) or more generally in the form of exclusive decision-making authority.

3. *How should the child's time (custody) be allotted between the co-parents' two homes?* This is the sticky wicket.

Personality Differences Among Co-Parents

The court can only define parenting and co-parenting responsibilities very broadly. With or without court orders, important differences between co-parents exist both as a function of personality and as a function of context.

"Personality" generally describes an individual's unique constellation of priorities, beliefs, practices, hopes, needs, and fears. These qualities gradually develop across the life span through adulthood as a result of some unknown mix of built-in predispositions called "temperament," unfolding genetic traits, experience, and determination. Above and beyond the familiar nature/nurture components, "determination" describes the concerted effort and gut-wrenching work that some people invest in personal change, as in the case of the young woman who is determined not to treat her children the way that her mother treated her.

Ironically, the very personality differences that can make an intimate partner attractive at the start of a relationship can become the source of the conflicts that end it. This is perhaps most often the case after a child enters the relationship, disturbing what was previously a workable, complementary balance. This all-too-common painful situation is made that much worse when the reality of the situation confirms the child's natural fears that he caused his parents' breakup.

Once conflict erupts, personality differences often become magnified and exploited (especially in the adversarial courts) in a self-fulfilling, downward spiral of destruction. The result can be that a relatively permissive man is cast as a selfish and neglectful father. A relatively strict mother is portrayed as rigid and abusive. One parent's temper begins to sound like dangerous rage, while the other parent's sensitivity is presented as disabling depression. Take medication? Suddenly you're an addict. Play the lottery? Now you're a gambler. Lose your job? You're a complete failure. Buying into these distortions can be self-validating but risks exposing the kids to inaccurate, damning, and destructive messages.

Differences Among Co-Parents Determined by Context: Are You the Parent-on-Duty (POD)?

Differences of personality might make one parent better with a child's practical needs (organizing homework, for example) and another better with a child's emotional needs (reassuring at bedtime). Differences of context can open or close the door on one or both parents' opportunities to bring these strengths to the job of parenting.

No matter whether co-parents live together or apart, no matter the legal status of the adult relationship, practical necessity will routinely place one parent there on the front line of parenting. Call this adult the "parent-on-duty" (POD).

Mom works days, and Dad works nights. Mom is the POD at breakfast and is responsible for getting the kids off to school each morning. Dad is the POD after school. He arranges snack, supervises homework, and sets limits on playtime. Dad has supper warming for Mom (his wife and co-parent) as he heads out to work and she returns for the night.

As in any relay, the baton of responsibility is passed. Dad relinquishes the POD role to Mom, who does baths and prayers and bedtime.

What if the intimate adult relationship fails? Let's say the co-parents live apart. They probably share legal decision-making authority. Perhaps residential responsibility is equally divided as well. The kids alternate homes, living one week with Dad in his new apartment and the next with Mom in her new condo. The parents' jobs haven't changed, but their co-parenting responsibilities have. Each is the POD for an entire week at a time, unrelieved by their former intimate partner.

Differences of context challenge caregivers personally and practically. For example, even if Dad could rearrange his work hours to be home on the mornings that the kids wake up in his apartment, he's never been an early morning kind of person. In addition to the practical (and very real financial) changes associated with his work, he'll also need to learn the skills necessary to get the kids off to school.

On the flip side of that same coin, Mom may discover that she can't change her work hours, which means either that the kids are home alone and unsupervised after school or that she needs to make other arrangements. For some co-parents, a mutual agreement that Dad can supervise the kids after school might make sense. For others, it may be best for Mom to arrange for a babysitter or nanny or to enroll the kids in an after-school program. Given that these important decisions bear on the children's well-being, Mom has at least a co-parenting responsibility (if not a legal obligation) to work out these details with Dad long before alerting the kids.

Differences of context, like differences of personality, are also prone to become magnified and distorted by conflicted co-parents. Consider the dilemma of the child whose weekdays are spent in his mother's care and whose weekends are spent in his father's care. As the POD during the school week, Mom has to set a great many more limits. Homework has to be completed. Rehearsals and music lessons and team practices have to be scheduled. Bedtime has to be enforced. She may find that she needs to create a lot of rules and associated consequences (hopefully emphasizing rewards for success whenever possible) about television and video games, phone and computer, bikes and skateboards.

Context allows Dad in this situation to be free and easy by comparison. He picks up his son after school Friday, and the two get to hang out until supper on Sunday. No homework. No lessons. Bedtime is relaxed. Add to this a spoonful of unresolved anger at his ex-wife and a cup or two of selfishness and guilt over the time away from his son, and Dad can easily begin to play into his son's wish to spend more time with him. Why not? It's all fun and games with Dad! Mom gets cast as the bad guy, and these differences become exaggerated until the child begins to refuse to return to Mom on Sundays and/or the co-parents end up back in court.

Differences Among Co-Parents Determined by Mutual Consent: Creating a Healthy and Reciprocal Division of Labor

When co-parents genuinely put their children's needs first, before their own, personality differences can be made into complementary parenting strengths. POD responsibilities associated with time and place can be defined so as to capitalize on these strengths, and open communication will help to mend holes in the child's safety net before any damage is done.

Working together as healthy and reciprocal co-parents is like tag-team wrestling. One of you enters the ring as POD to respond to the child's need. Practicing the violin? Pitching a softball? Eating his vegetables? Flushing the toilet? Going on her first date? Recovering from surgery? If that parent's effort falls short, if the need persists or a different approach might work better, the other parent is tagged in. Sometimes co-parents need to double-team the child. Other times the co-parents need to tag in an auxiliary parenting partner: a teacher or tutor, babysitter or therapist, physician, neighbor, uncle, or grandparent. So long as the co-parenting team remains focused on the child's needs, communicating and cooperating respectfully, the outlook for the child is promising.

Grades are falling since Dad assumed POD responsibilities after school? Okay. Maybe Dad's not terribly organized, he's too tired at the end of his workday, or he doesn't have the background to help with calculus. If the focus is on the child's needs, then perhaps the schedule should be changed so that Mom is the POD after school, or Dad and Mom should agree to hire a tutor.

The ten-year-old risks being kicked off the swim team because Mom can't get her there on Saturdays? If Mom is a cooperative, child-centered caregiver, she tags Dad in and asks him to do the transportation. This might mean that father and daughter have an additional morning together for the duration of the swim season, or that larger changes in the parenting plan are negotiated to facilitate the child's needs.

Does this mean that court-ordered parenting responsibilities and limitations should be ignored? Not at all, but even co-parents who have needed and received court-ordered parenting plans can usually change those plans by mutual agreement, seeking the court's endorsement of such changes whenever necessary.

Chapter 3

What If You're a Single Parent?

As common as divorce is, single parents are really quite rare.

You may be an *unmarried parent*. Because the biological processes of conception and birth have no necessary connection to the legal/religious/political processes of marriage, millions of unmarried adults (and, tragically, teenagers as well) have children every day. This does not make you a single parent.

A "single parent" is an adult who shares caregiving responsibilities for a child with no one at all. None of the willing and available relatives, neighbors, friends, or community members who might otherwise share the primary caregiver's burdens and complement her resources play any significant role in caring for her child. This lonely and limiting circumstance can be the result either of seemingly insurmountable differences between a parent's beliefs and behaviors and those of the surrounding community, a parent's extreme depression and anxiety, or—only rarely—an actual absence of real supports.

Taking Off the Training Wheels

The simple fact is that we live in a very scary world. The constant flow of media keeps us hyperaware of all of the dangers that surround us, such as school shootings and terrorism, global warming and pollution, product recalls, sexual predators, and tainted produce.

But we also live in a world that is full of beauty and promise. There are people who give selflessly, opportunities for growth and innovation, and creative expressions that dazzle the senses and open doors into ever more creative and wonderful experiences.

No doubt your children are the most precious parts of your life. It's not unusual for parents to say that their children *are* their life. Of course you want to protect them. But we must never allow our protections to cause our children harm.

A healthy parent's goal is to raise a child who can go off into the world on his own. We can only succeed in this goal by carefully allowing our kids to cope with bigger and bigger realities. The child who never goes out into the world cannot become an adult who is ready to face it.

Think about how you taught (or will someday teach) your daughter to ride a two-wheel bicycle. You ran alongside as far as you could or as far as she'd allow, holding on to the bike to keep her steady. If you never let go, she'd never fall, but neither would she ever learn to ride on her own. As a healthy parent you do your best to judge when to let go, knowing that she'll fall and

Taking Off the Training Wheels *(continued)*

perhaps even get hurt. But you and she both know that you'll be there to comfort her, to bandage the boo-boo, and to send her back out to try again.

No matter the circumstance, raising a child alone puts the single parent and the child at risk. Lacking support and validation, respite and perspective, the adult trying to raise a child unassisted is vulnerable to burnout. Co-parents give one another a chance to step away from the intense emotions of caregiving, to get themselves refueled, and to learn by talking through recent events. Lacking co-parents entirely, the single parent quickly becomes exhausted, losing patience and the emotional distance that helps us anchor our children and weave that safety net beneath them. Like burnout of any kind, attempting to raise a child unassisted is a recipe for anger and conflict, depression and anxiety.

Perhaps more important than the price the adult pays for trying to raise a child unassisted is the price the child must pay for her parent's solitude. The child of a single parent has no model from which to learn mature compromise and cooperation, conflict and conflict resolution. The child of a single parent has no backup plan: her safety net is being held up by a single pair of hands. Lacking all but one caregiver's example, this child may always feel insecure. She may struggle her whole life to adapt to change, to develop healthy empathy and cognitive flexibility. Most powerfully, the child of an isolated, single parent is at risk for compromising her childhood by becoming adultified.

If you are a single parent—if you genuinely have no peer support, validation, or relief—you must reach out for help. You must begin to build a co-parenting team. This has nothing to do with whether or not you choose to explore intimate adult relationships. It has nothing to do with sexuality or gender. It has everything to do with your child's well-being.

Raising a healthy child does, indeed, take a village. The first step might be asking a physician or mental health professional for help with the anxiety, depression, or whatever other condition has isolated you. It might mean asking a religious leader for assistance either in finding like-minded others or in better fitting into the surrounding culture without compromising your beliefs. It might mean knocking on the door across the hall or joining an Internet chat room or listserv. No matter what first step makes most sense to you, you must take one. Beginning to build a co-parenting team may be scary. It will require a great deal of inner strength, and it may even mean changing your lifestyle and taking risks that you've never taken before.

You've taken the first step already. You're reading these pages. Now go one step further. Reach out and trust one other adult today. Make a play date for your kids together. Share a story about parenting. Ask for an opinion. Your child is worth it.

Chapter 4

Row, Row, Row Your Boat

One way to understand the promise and the perils of co-parenting is to imagine that you and your co-parent are seated side by side in a rowboat, each with an oar. Your job is to work together to get the boat to shore. No matter how rough the seas, you will always have a better chance of reaching your goal if you row together, synchronize your efforts, and communicate about your progress. Working as a team, one partner can rest while the other pulls on both oars. When waves or weather push the boat off course, negotiation and compromise allow for corrections.

The problems arise when communication fails. Without adequate communication, you and your co-parent may be working against one another. Without mutual support, one or both partners quickly become resentful and exhausted. Without mutual trust and respect, blame, shame, guilt, and anger will sink the boat, and with it goes the child.

Consider, for example, the case of Jack and Jill. Rowing side by side,

Jack believes that Jill is leaning too far to port, away from him, causing the boat to list and wander off course. Rather than say anything, Jack decides to correct the problem by leaning to starboard. He worries that Jill will be angered by his feedback. Of course, Jill feels Jack's weight leaning away from her and decides that she needs to lean farther to port. She's worried that Jack will resent her observation. Without communication, stumbling over their egos and misassumptions, this polarizing process goes on until they both fall overboard, the boat is lost, and the child is caught in the middle.

Been there? Done that?

Dad believes that Mom is too harsh, so he becomes more lenient. Instead of saying something to his parenting partner, he subtly tries to make up for her. Mom sees that Dad has become a pushover, so she buckles down. She thinks that he'll take her feedback as criticism and overreact, so she says nothing. Gradually, the split between the two widens and widens, one becoming extremely permissive while the other becomes ever more rigid and authoritarian. As the inconsistencies grow, so do the holes in the emotional safety net that is supposed to hold their precious and beloved child, leaving him nervous and fearful, angry, and out of control.

Weaving a Safety Net Together

This is the goal: You and your co-parents will work together to weave a safety net beneath your child. The tools with which you create this safety net are simple. Chances are good that you learned them in grade school. Perhaps your parents modeled them for you as well: communication, cooperation, and compromise. The more constructive, proactive, and child-centered the two of you are together, the tighter the weave and the more secure the child. The more selfish, unilateral, and closed you are, the more holes will appear and the more insecure your kids will feel.

"Me?" you're protesting. "I communicate! I cooperate! It's my kids' other parent who doesn't!"

Good. It's important that you do everything you can, that you take the high road whenever possible, but it's not enough. Your defensive posture turns this into a me-versus-my-co-parent dilemma. It creates a hole that will swallow your kids in an instant. From your child's point of view, what matters is not who is cooperating and who is not, but whether the team works and whether the safety net is intact.

From your child's point of view, it's not about who is the better parent. It's about building a secure foundation of self.

A secure child is more likely to have the social and emotional resources to learn and explore, to make friends and try new experiences, to adapt to change, to cope with frustration and failure, and to put his needs second to others' when necessary.

A child who has the good fortune to have co-parents who are mature and cooperative goes out into the world confident, able, and willing to develop her own healthy, reciprocal relationships.

A child whose parents put their own needs first—whose communication falters or fails and whose consistency is poor—a child whose parents each need to be better than the other, may never feel secure. That child may be destined to establish adult relationships that re-create the same emotional holes she lived with as a child and to pass these on in turn to her own children.

Human beings are confusing in this situation. Given a limit, we usually feel compelled to test it (review this concept in the Introduction).
Draw a line in the sand, and tell your son not to cross it. What will he
do? More or less subtly, more or less defiantly, he'll put a toe over that
line and wait to see what happens. If you respond calmly and predictably and firmly, he may not be happy, but he'll learn to stay on his
side of the line. He'll feel secure and reassured. The safety net held. If
your reaction is full of emotion, inconsistent, or wishy-washy, sooner or
later he'll put his foot over the line, then his leg, and then he'll be
singing with joy, "Look what I got away with!" but he'll feel insecure,
anxious, and uncontained.

When co-parents are inconsistent, when disrespect and adult feelings cripple communication and rip holes in your child's safety net, he
will pick at it until it's larger, taking advantage of the split until he
escapes, celebrating his freedom almost as much as it scares him.

Chapter 5

The Essentials of Co-Parenting

I f our job as co-parents is to create an emotional safety net beneath our kids, these are the conceptual threads—the warp and weft—with which we weave:

1. *Health and safety are always our first priority.* As often as we are forced to choose between that which makes our kids happy and that which makes our kids healthy, we always choose health first. Choices that compromise our children's health to make them happy are self-serving and short-lived. Choices that help our children become healthy allow them to discover their own happiness.

2. *Our love for our children is forever and no matter what.* We know that our kids will test our limits, defy our rules, damage our possessions, and maybe even lash out in rage. Their specific behaviors may not be acceptable, but our love for our children is unbreakable. This is especially important when parents separate. While it appears that love can stop, your love for your child will not.

3. *We always promote our children's relationship with our co-parents.* We do this by speaking to and about one another with respect. We never allow our adult feelings for one another (or any other adult's words or actions) to hinder the quality of our kids' relationships with each of us.

4. *We know that every person needs to feel loved and accepted.* As adults, we do everything we can to make sure that our emotional needs are met by other adults. As parents, we expect and accept that we will provide love and acceptance for our children without any expectation in return.

5. *We know that our own health and calm, firm presence reassure our children.* We take every reasonable step to remain physically and emotionally healthy and to learn to be the best caregivers we can. In doing so, we are not only giving our kids a solid foundation upon which they can grow, but we are also giving them permission through our example to take good care of themselves.

Living Together in Conflict

The goal is *not* to live without conflict.

Conflict is an expectable part of any caring relationship. The anger, fear, and sadness that fuel conflict are as necessary and natural as the happiness, hopes, and dreams that create the unique fabric of each relationship.

Because conflict happens, the goal is to manage it in healthy ways so that it becomes an opportunity for growth rather than a weapon of destruction. It's far easier to reach this goal when the relationship affects no one but you and your intimate adult partner. Once a child enters the equation, managing conflict in healthy ways can become at least as difficult as it is important.

What we know with certainty is that our kids are the barometers of our adult relationships. When we feel content, loved, and accepted, the emotional pressure in our lives diminishes, and our kids feel safe, confident, and secure. When conflict erupts in our adult relationships, the emotional pressure increases, and our kids feel anxious and fearful. Their behavior becomes less mature (a process known as regression), their emotions become erratic, and, over time, their sense of themselves and their ability to develop their own healthy relationships can be damaged.

"My daughter's too young to understand."

"My son has learning and attention difficulties. When we argue, it goes right over his head."

"My teenager is off in his own little world. He doesn't know."

These are among the excuses that conflicted co-parents commonly make in the interest of comforting themselves. Unfortunately, all three are wrong. We know, for example, that newborn infants respond differently to the emotional tone of the voices that surround them and to the different physical experiences of being held by a calm parent or by an angry parent. Long before words are understood, the visual, audible, and tactile experiences of emotional pressure can cause a child to become tense herself, to cry and refuse food, or become unable to hold it down. When the pressure persists, physical development can be impacted and emotional development thrown off course. The child can become overly clingy or begin to reject caregiving altogether. In the long term, exposure to continuous emotional pressure can cause an infant or a toddler to shut down in something known as conservation-withdrawal.

We know as well that kids who struggle with math and English and science in school, those who are diagnosed with attention problems or with learning differences (including nonverbal learning disabilities), and even those on the autistic spectrum (Asperger's syndrome, for example) read and respond to their caregiver's emotions as much as their age mates, even if they are less able to put their experience into words.

And your teenager with his face buried in a video screen and his ears submersed in rap 'n' roll? Yep, he's listening, too. In fact, you have to wonder how much of some kids' escape into digital media, sports, drugs and alcohol, peer groups, and gangs are a response to the tension they live with at home.

The simple fact is that you cannot hide your feelings from your kids. They get it. They feel the conflict in your intimate adult relationship even if they don't see or hear it, and it affects them. Whether their experience of your adult conflict teaches them healthy strategies for coping with their own inevitable conflicts or leaves them scared, needy, angry, and confused depends on many factors, not the least of which is your success in keeping them out of the middle.

All in the Family

Kids become drawn into their parents' conflicts in a million subtle ways. The dramatic examples are easy to identify: the divorced mom who asks her son to collect the support check from his dad, the bitter partners who try to recruit their daughter into their hatred for each other, or the depressed dad who enlists his son to care for the younger kids— even the well-intentioned divorced couple who give their children the freedom to come and go at will between their two neighboring homes.

The most common ways that co-parents draw their kids into the middle are no less harmful, but they are much harder to see. These are the subtle, quiet, and usually well-intentioned ways in which that safety net woven between two caregivers is slowly torn to shreds. They can be classified into five types.

When was the last time you made one of these mistakes?

1. *Arguing about consequences in front of the kids.* Perhaps the most common trap that co-parents fall into sounds like this:

   "Billy," one caregiver says, "that behavior is unacceptable! You're grounded for a month!"

   "Just a minute," the other caregiver replies, right there in front of the child. "That's way too harsh. I think he should only be grounded for a week!"

   Suddenly, the conflict has shifted from the child and one parent to the two co-parents, leaving Billy on the sidelines, stirred up with feelings about the unacceptable behavior, and now amplified by the fact that he's caused (yet another) fight between his parents. This is a recipe for disaster.

   "I already gave him a consequence!"

   "And I'm changing it! I'm his father, and I'm in charge. Billy, it's only a week!

   Father, in this instance, may have changed Billy's punishment, but much more significantly, he undermined Mother's authority. What will happen next time Mom tries to punish Billy? Right: Billy will run to Dad. Mom has lost respect and control. A subtle alliance between Billy and Dad has been built against Mom.

In a healthier interaction, Mom would have enforced an existing consequence. Last time Billy did something similar, an expectation had been set: "If it happens again, then . . ." This not only makes the world predictable for Billy, but makes it much more likely that the parent-on-duty will be supported by the other parent later.

Even without the benefit of this prior structure to fall back on, Dad could have questioned Mom later, away from Billy. If that discussion helps Mom to change her mind, she has time to go back to Billy to correct herself: "I think I was too harsh, Billy. Here's what we're going to do . . ."

Or there is another choice. As long as everyone is safe, the POD (Mom, in this instance) could simply have said, "You're grounded until your father and I can talk it through. We'll let you know what the long-term consequence will be."

But if Dad felt compelled to take a stand there and then in front of Billy, at least he could have done so in a respectful way:

"Hold on a second, Martha. Do you think that might be a little too much?"

"Hmmm . . . I hear you, George. Maybe I am overreacting a bit. What do you think would work better?"

This process has the benefit of modeling healthy compromise and negotiation, even though it still risks casting one parent as the good guy and the other as the bad guy in front of the child. The result, formulated on the spot by mutually respectful, child-centered co-parents, sounds like, "Okay, Billy. Your dad and I agree. You're grounded for ten days."

2. *Undoing your co-parent's consequences.* Consistency calls for co-parents to communicate in the interest of enforcing similar limits and consequences between homes when the co-parents live apart. Stability and predictability call for follow-through over time. When communication fails and consistency is poor, co-parents can become pitted against one another in the good-guy and bad-guy roles, a schism that leaves their child stuck in the middle.

Let's change the story of Billy's grounding just a little. In this version, the parents live apart. Dad wasn't present when Mom and Billy argued. It's only the next day, after Billy transitions between homes that the situation comes to Dad's attention:

"Your mom grounded you for a month? Nah, don't listen to her. You know how she gets all emotional. Let's make it three days instead."

Dad has undermined Mom's authority. He's created an alliance with his son against his co-parent, very likely for selfish reasons. He's also put Billy in the middle of their argument by not even communicating the fact directly to his parenting partner that he commuted the child's sentence!

3. *"The cat's away, so the mice will play."* Consistency among caregivers means that co-parents work to maintain similar expectations and consequences. Consistency is one form of structure that helps to decrease anxiety and defuse conflict.

"The cat's away, so the mice will play" refers to one parent's knowing wink to the child that says about another parent, "Okay, the bad guy's gone. Go ahead . . ."

To some people, this is the stereotyped overindulgent grandparent. Dad spends twenty minutes filling his own mother in on the structure in the home before he leaves for a business trip, but loving, doting Grandma thinks that Dad's too tough. She never gets to see her grandkids anyway, and she has no intention of wasting a few precious days alone with them enforcing his silly rules. Rather than say anything, however, she pretends to listen carefully, taking every opportunity to share that knowing wink with the kids.

This story doesn't have to be about Grandma coming to visit for three days each year. It could just as easily be about one of a pair of parents who share the children full time. There's something cute and endearing about the idea of a mom or dad saying something like, "Daddy's gone. Now we can have fun." But in this case, cute and endearing mask selfish and destructive. The message here is, "He's the bad guy. He interferes with our fun!" The opportunity to giggle and laugh and break the rules while the cat's away is enticing, but a wedge has been driven between the co-parents.

4. *Keeping secrets and secret alliances.* Secrets are destructive. Asking a child to keep a secret can be like asking her to carry around a load of bricks. It's a burden that demands an enormous amount of her strength. It will inevitably crash to the floor, and someone will get hurt.

When one caregiver asks a child to keep a secret from another, an alliance is established that can undermine the child's relationship with the other parent and the quality of the co-parenting relationship. The message to the child is exciting and scary all at once: "You and I share something special that your other parent can't know." This is an invitation to the child to share other secrets with her new ally and keep those same secrets from the other parent, gradually building a wall with the allied parent on one side and the left-out parent on the other.

5. *"Wait until your father gets home!"* This is a familiar rant, a parenting cop-out reminiscent of the 1950s, a chauvinistic era when mothers took a backseat to fathers in everything that occurred outside of the kitchen. In our contemporary world, the caregiver who defers authority to her co-parent (regardless of gender) is setting herself up for the child's disrespect and setting her co-parent up to be the bad guy. The message is, "I feel helpless and can't stop you, but your other parent will come to the rescue!"

There are certainly situations in which the POD feels ineffective and powerless. Chief among these are the very scary situations that can arise when a teenager's behavior becomes violent. When safety is at issue (when violence or threats of violence arise, when behavior is destructive, or there is a risk of runaway, as examples), calling in support may be necessary. This means calling in a co-parent and, in the extreme, the police and/or emergency medical providers (calling 911 or going to the local hospital emergency room).

When Parents Need Police

Firm limits and predictable consequences are nowhere more important than when safety is at issue. Anything that threatens to cause physical harm, many things that threaten to cause destruction of property, and certain high-risk behaviors including running away and the illegal use of drugs and alcohol are safety concerns. Be clear now with your co-parent and your kids that there will be zero tolerance for these and similar behaviors.

What does this mean? For many co-parents, this approach means simply that the police will be notified immediately. Call your local police department today (the seven- or ten-digit number, not the emergency number), or ask your teen to make the call herself. Ask what they do when a parent alerts them to a teen's unsafe behavior. By establishing this contingency now, you are acting to assure safety and enforcing your zero-tolerance standard.

Does reaching out to a co-parent or the police mean that you're passing the buck, or that you're deferring authority to someone else, making yourself into the good guy or ducking responsibility? Done correctly, it will not. It means that you're asking for assistance. You're getting help to make sure that the kids' safety net is held firmly and tightly woven. Rather than "Wait until your father gets home!" your position becomes, "This is important enough that I need my co-parents and supports on board here and now."

Pop Quiz: What Are You Feeling?

Can you tell the difference between your experience of these four basic feelings: happy, sad, mad, and scared? Surprisingly many people don't know that they're having any feeling until it explodes. Many others can distinguish only between the experience of happy and upset, but nothing further.

But go one step further. Ask yourself *how much* emotion you're experiencing, on a scale of one to ten. "How full is my emotion balloon?" As pressure builds toward ten on a ten-point scale, mature, rational decision-making abilities diminish until you're bound to explode in impulsive, destructive words and actions.

Give yourself (and your partner) pop quizzes throughout the day. The goal is to learn to recognize what you're feeling and how much of it you're feeling—how full the balloon is—during the relatively calm and quiet times so that you're better prepared for those yelling-screaming-conflicted-ten-out-of-ten explosive times.

"Take the High Road":
How Do You Cope with Conflict?

You must always take the high road—making the healthiest choices that you can, no matter what your co-parent does. To do otherwise means lowering yourself to your co-parent's level, participating in a downward spiral of escalating distrust and rage that will settle nothing and harm no one more than your child.

Easier said than done, right? Right. So here's the beginner's guide to taking the high road. Taking these steps yourself is a great start. Taking these steps together with your co-parent is the ideal:

1. *Learn to recognize your own emotional experience.* Feelings are as real as the air that fills a balloon, creating pressure that must sooner or later find release. Too many of us are guilty of minimizing and denying our emotional experience until the balloon explodes. Ignoring the building pressures can only ever be a short-term solution, albeit a necessary solution in some situations (with the boss, perhaps). Taking the high road means learning to acknowledge at least to yourself—and, better still, out loud in acceptable language—what you're feeling and how much of it you're feeling at any given time.

Here's some vocabulary that might help. What words would you add to these descriptions?

How Much Pressure in the Balloon?	Happy	Sad	Mad	Scared
1				
2	Pleased	Disappointed	Frustrated	Nervous
3				
4			Annoyed	
5	Content	Down	Aggravated	Worried
6			Angry	
7	Joyous		Furious	Anxious
8				
9				
10	Ecstatic	Grief stricken	Enraged	Terrified

2. *Learn how to let the pressure out of the balloon.* Plan ahead. Establish healthy and acceptable emotional outlets now, while things are calm and you're thinking clearly, in advance of the powerful feelings that are bound to erupt later. Saying what is *not* okay to do when you're angry is not enough. It's far more important to establish in advance what *is* okay to do with strong feelings.

The best expressions of feelings let the air out of the balloon long before it reaches ten. What can you do when the balloon reaches three? Five? Seven? Early on, while emotion is still moderate and mature thinking hasn't yet been washed away, it will always be best to express the feelings directly and constructively in words: "I'm really annoyed that . . ."

And what do you do if the emotional pressure approaches ten? You should plan ahead now for that likelihood as well. What behaviors are acceptable outlets? Can you walk around the block? Punch a pillow? Shred yesterday's newspaper? Scream into an empty milk jug or two-liter bottle? Throw a snowball at a tree?

Establishing release valves in advance with your parenting partner will not only help the two of you cope with conflict in healthier ways, it creates a valuable model that your kids will learn to emulate. The following chart illustrates one family's anger expression plan:

How Much Pressure?	How Best to Vent
1	Talk it out directly: "I feel . . ."
2	Talk it out directly: "I feel . . ."
3	Talk it out directly: "I feel . . ."
4	Talk it out directly: "I feel . . ."
5	Talk it out directly: "I feel . . ."
6	Take ten to calm down before talking
7	Take ten to calm down before talking
8	Physical outlets to vent: jog, exercise
9	Physical outlets to vent: jog, exercise
10	Physical outlets to vent: jog, exercise

3. *Learn how to fight fair.* Learning to acknowledge and appropriately vent emotional pressure is necessary, but not sufficient. You and your parenting partner need to go at least one step further. You need to learn what it means to fight fair.

Fighting fair means responding to a person's behavior, not to the person himself. It means not calling names, not damaging property, and never acting violently or threatening violence. Feelings that are strong enough to prompt behavior that breaks things or hurts people (the balloon is more than half full and close to exploding) need to be vented elsewhere, away from the conflict, before any direct exchange can begin to be constructive.

Fighting fair means following critical responses ("I hate it when you . . .") with constructive suggestions ("Next time I'd appreciate it if you would . . ."). It means listening openly and accepting feedback. It means taking time to acknowledge your partner's feelings ("I understand that I made you mad"), to agree to think through their feedback ("Let me sleep on it"), and then following through later ("I thought about what you said, and I can try. . .").

Fighting fair means addressing one issue at a time, taking care not to allow a single incident to generalize into an argument about everything that has ever annoyed you. It means taking one subject at a time without countering with a quid pro quo ("If you're going to complain about this, then I'm going to complain about that!") or a childish, "But you started it!"

Perhaps most important, fighting fair means keeping the kids out of the middle. It means never asking the kids to take sides, never asking them to validate one adult position or invalidate another. It means never unnecessarily exposing the kids to adult conflict. If, however, the kids are exposed, fighting fair means acknowledging that the conflict is real ("Your dad and I are having an argument"), reassuring them that all is well ("Everyone argues sometimes; we always love one another"), and letting them witness the argument's closure at least as much as they witnessed the conflict itself. Too many co-parents argue openly but make up behind closed doors, a dilemma that can leave kids worried that the conflict persists.

4. *Get help when it's needed.* Healthy coping and child-centered co-parenting often require assistance. Far from being a sign of weakness, asking a neighbor, friend, relative coworker, clergyperson, physician, or therapist to hear your story is the best way to let some of the emotional pressure out of the balloon before trying to address the concern directly. Talking through your upset will help you organize your thinking, gain perspective on your strong feelings, better understand the other person's choices and feelings, and determine when and how best to bring up the concerns.

   Beware that asking family or friends for help with a relationship conflict might leave that person feeling caught in the middle. Different from putting your kids in the middle, the adults whom you seek out as helpers presumably have the maturity to decline being put in an awkward situation. Should they agree to help, they have the maturity and objectivity to address the situation constructively and without fear of personal consequences or reprisals.

Asking for help doesn't need to be a secret. Letting your co-parent know that you've reached out for assistance can be an important step toward breaking through denial, minimalization, and resistance. Letting the kids know that you have a helper gives them permission to ask for help when they need it as well.

When you and your co-parent have tried and failed to address critical concerns, asking for help together—as a co-parenting team—can make all the difference. A marital or couples therapist, a mediator or co-parenting facilitator, a guardian ad litem, parenting coordinator or—in those most extreme situations—a judge can help you voice your concern constructively and reach a conclusion that suits the children's needs, even if it may be contrary to your own wishes.

Chapter 6

The Child's Experience
of Adult Conflict

I t doesn't matter whether you live together or apart, whether you're married, never married, separated, or divorced. It doesn't matter whether you and your co-parent are intimate adult partners, friends or enemies, or parent and child yourselves. If you are co-parents, you are mutually responsible for creating the foundation upon which your child is building his self.

"Self?" Psychologists call it "ego." Either term refers to the internal experience related to the word "I." Self is an accumulation of perceptions and experiences, strengths and weaknesses, and skills and hopes and fears. It is somewhere between the image we see in the bathroom mirror each morning and the image we want to see in the mirror—a collection of beliefs that guides our thinking, shapes our feelings, and determines our behavior throughout the day.

Imagine that growing up is like constructing a tower, one story at a time, one developmental floor before the next. The foreman has orders to impress the neighbors, so she determines that construction must focus on the exterior. Floors are added and façades are created that will win admiration early on from parents ("Good job, sweetie!") as the building gets higher, or an "Awesome, dude!" from peers. Spotlights, marquees, and billboards go up long before the carpets, woodwork, and trim go in, some for the purpose of hiding the scars, weaknesses, and fears discovered along the way.

By the time a child is two or three years old, his squat little office building of a self seems cute and adorable. We visit it often ("Look, Mommy!") to applaud its new structures and to hold up the newest beams and girders while the child welds them in place ("Try again, sweetie! You can do it!"). By the teenage years, the same structure looms nearly as large and impressive as many of the adult skyscrapers that surround it. We visit less often ("Will you be home for supper?") and do our best to respect the new workers who have joined the crew ("I'm going over to Suzie's to do social studies, okay?").

Tourists flock to see the new building as it goes up ("Look how he's grown!"), applauding and admiring and gawking in amazement. To them, the building that is your child's emerging self is incredibly impressive, but as a parent, you can see through the façade. You know that the hallways are mostly bare and circuitous and poorly lit, at best. You know that the wiring sometimes short-circuits and that the plumbing often overflows and that the elevators tend to go down much more often than they go up.

And the foundation?

Whether the foundation of your child's growing self rests on footers sunk deep into the bedrock of emotional security or upon cracked cinderblocks laid carelessly in the shifting sands of anxiety, anger, and depression depends largely on you and your co-parents. She'll hire decorators and designers and electricians to finish those interior rooms later. What matters now, in childhood, is the integrity of the foundation upon which the structure is being built: the quality of your co-parenting relationship.

Your child experiences the quality of your co-parenting relationship in the deepest foundations of her self. The co-parents' mutual success in communicating, putting the child's needs first, and providing her with consistency and support from the earliest moments of life onward will help determine how she weathers the emotional stresses ahead.

Children have different experiences of their parents' conflicts. For some, Mom and Dad's bickering, anger, inconsistencies, and failed communications are as harmless as a summer shower. For others, the same events strike like hail. The structure of self sustains some superficial damage—broken windows and lost roof tiles—but the foundation remains untouched. For others still—those most constitutionally vulnerable, exposed to conflict the longest, or most deeply scarred—these same events are experienced as tsunami-like damage, razing the entire structure or creating deep fault lines that leave the building vulnerable to later assaults.

The differences between these children and their experiences of co-parental conflict are due to a combination of at least two factors: how long and how severe the adult conflict has been and the presence of concurrent resources and vulnerabilities.

By now it should be clear that the child's experience of the adult conflict begins long before it becomes public. Imagining that the conflict begins when the divorce papers are filed is as foolish as saying that your education begins when you receive your diploma.

We must understand that the child's experience of tension in the home begins long before legal papers are filed and long before the adults move apart. It began long before the last argument and perhaps even long before the first argument. It was there in the air, as quiet and poisonous as carbon monoxide. From your child's point of view—the reality that matters most—the co-parenting conflict dates back to those early, tense silences, no matter how much you may have pretended that everything was okay. It dates back to his first experience of loud voices (remember how he used to plug his ears and scream for you to stop yelling?), of slammed doors and angry words.

From your child's point of view, the conflict is as old as his first confusion hearing one thing from Mom and another from Dad. It's as old as the time one parent asked him to tell the other parent something, as old as the first time he heard one loving and beloved parent damn the other aloud.

From your child's point of view, the adult conflict goes back beyond that first terrifying, gut-wrenching, and heartbreaking night when he suddenly had to decide whether to leave with Mom or stay with Dad.

The earlier and longer lasting a child's experience of co-parental conflict, the greater the potential that he will suffer serious emotional harm. The resulting harm may be as obvious as an earthquake or invisible, like a fault in the foundation of self waiting for later relationships to split it apart.

Fortunately, the flip side of the coin is also true. The longer a child has the opportunity to grow up with the benefit of a tightly woven safety net—a solid co-parenting foundation—beneath him, the better he will weather later co-parenting conflicts and his own relationship struggles. A child's experience of cooperative co-parent communication, consistency, and child-centered decision-making reinforces the foundations of self, instilling security, confidence, and a healthy model upon which to build his own later, collaborative relationships.

Beware of the innumerable exceptions and qualifications to these very general rules, such as biological predispositions; medical vulnerabilities; the role of other, simultaneous stressors; and the supportive role of concurrent resources and vulnerabilities: those intellectual, social, and emotional factors that can either help to protect a child from the potential emotional harm he might otherwise endure due to co-parental conflict or that can leave him raw, exposed, and at greater risk.

Assessing a Child's Resources and Risk Factors

The emotional harm that a child experiences as a result of co-parental conflict can be minimized when some factors are present (resources) and magnified when other factors are present (risk factors). Some of these factors are listed on page 68.

In general, children cope best with stress when stability and familiarity are maximized, when healthy habits are reinforced, and when they have the skills and opportunities necessary to understand and talk about their experiences as they occur. Some of these factors may be out of the control of even the most well-intentioned and resourceful caregivers: a child's chronic physical or mental illness, court-ordered

Resources	Risk Factors
Caregivers are careful not to unnecessarily expose the child to the conflict or put him in the middle.	One or both caregivers needlessly expose the child to their conflict and/or put him in the middle.
Regular physical exercise, healthy diet, and good sleep.	No exercise, interrupted exercise routine, poor diet and sleep.
Continuous contact with a caring adult outside of the family conflict (e.g., trusted therapist, clergy, coach, or teacher).	Loss of contact with a previously caring adult outside the family conflict (e.g., trusted therapist, clergy, coach, or teacher).
Continuous contact with a familiar and supportive group, club, or organization (e.g., Scouts, football team, religious group).	Loss of contact with a previously familiar and supportive group, club, organization, or team.
Continuous participation in a rewarding and pleasurable activity (e.g., music, theater, dance, sports).	Physical illness, injury, or intervention (and some medications).
Opportunities to engage others socially.	Social isolation.
Intelligence, especially strong verbal comprehension and expressive skills.	Mental illness (especially anxiety and depression).
Familiarity with peers who have endured co-parental conflict.	Significant loss (especially death of a loved one).
The absence of mental illness, learning, physical, or developmental difference.	Introduction of a new family member.
Enjoys creative outlets, (drawing, poetry, music, dance).	Relocation to a new home or change of school.

changes that interrupt stability and continuity, and constitutional limitations impacting intelligence or expressive skills. Others among these factors can be engineered by co-parents who are mature enough to put their children's needs first: a stable home and school, continuity of important relationships and affiliations, healthy habits, and expressive outlets.

Chief among the resources that co-parents can provide to their children is the opportunity to establish and maintain a healthy relationship with a nurturing adult outside of the co-parental conflict. Sometimes a teacher, coach, or Scout leader can play this role. Other times a child therapist may be more appropriate.

Chapter 7

A Quick Word About Promises

A s much as conflict in an intimate adult relationship can be blindingly painful, as parents we must always be aware of how our choices impact our children. Thus we should do everything that we can—within reason—to minimize the pain that our children must endure as we struggle with our adult relationships.

In the heat of an emotional moment, it's all too easy to make promises that you can't keep, to offer your child reassurances in the interest of calming down or getting through a tough time, or, selfishly, to quell your guilt or be reassured of a child's love when adult love has failed.

"I promise that I'll see you Wednesday."

"I promise that we'll all be together."

"I promise that this will all be okay."

To us as parents and adults, these and similar statements are usually meant as general aspirations, as fleeting words filling passing moments. To children who tend to think more concretely, especially when under stress, these words are lifelines thrown into stormy seas.

Expect that your kids are listening very closely and that they take your words very literally and will remember them for a very long time.

Making promises that you can't keep costs trust. When a child's basic emotional security is threatened, when the safety net that she counts on is tearing apart, her ability to trust in you may be among her last threads of hope. The short-term gain of an empty promise is not worth the long-term cost of trust and hope and the resulting anger and sadness.

There is, however, one promise that you can and should make often. It may not settle a particular upset entirely, but it should help. It's a promise that your co-parent can never undo, that the court can never change, and when all is said and done, it's the most important promise that your child will ever need to hear:

"I promise that I love you, no matter what."

Should We Split Up?

If the decision to stay together or split up impacted no one but you and your partner—two adults who are presumably mature enough to make decisions and cope with the consequences—then you could do as you like. Stay together today. Break up tomorrow. Get back together in a week or a month or a decade.

Some people live this way, changing partners like square dancers on a Saturday night, staying with one as long as it feels good and splitting up when the pressures outnumber the

Should We Split Up? *(continued)*

pleasures, when the conflicts become too big and too frequent. Moral objections and medical concerns aside, there's nothing inhcrently wrong with this.

Once a child enters the picture, however, the stakes go up dramatically. The self-centered interests that once determined your choices have to take a backseat to the child's interests. This requires maturity: a selfless willingness to delay personal gratification and to tolerate frustration in the service of the child's health and happiness.

Sadly, the physical maturity necessary to have a child routinely develops years before the emotional maturity necessary to raise a child.

Chapter 8

The Myth of the Nuclear Family

H istory, culture, religion, and the media have implicitly con-
spired to promote the myth of the nuclear family. According to
this myth, family is composed of a father, mother, and their
children. Period. Children raised in this *Leave It to
Beaver*-type environment are healthy and strong. They become cap-
tains of the football team and cheerleaders. They grow up behind white
picket fences, go to Ivy League colleges, marry one another, and live
happily ever after.

This is a pleasant story about a world that some might find desirable,
but it is not the world outside my window. It's probably not the world
outside yours either.

Much as it does, indeed, take a village to raise a child, an intact
nuclear family is not necessary for the job to be done right. Healthy
children are raised every day by never-married or divorced parents of
both genders living alone, living with same-gender partners, or living

with extended family. Healthy children have grown up for centuries in the cooperative care of scores of unrelated caregivers in communes, Israeli kibbutzim, and African longhouses.

Some healthy children know their birth parents; others never meet them.

The myth of the nuclear family is just that: a myth. It's a story that once validated the lives of a majority of white, middle-class Americans and gave them reason to disparage all the other varieties of family. This story today illustrates only one lifestyle among the many that healthy parents might choose.

Family composition does not determine a child's health. Far more important is the child's experience of unconditional love, firm and consistent limits, and a safety net woven tightly among the loving adults who share his care.

Staying Together for the Kids

Don't. It's that simple.

The idea of staying together for the kids is the ultimate act of putting the kids in the middle. It is an unhealthy and destructive reversal of roles, making the children responsible not only for the adults' well-being but for the family's continuing existence.

After you and your intimate adult partner have exhausted every resource and every intervention, support, and therapy—after you dig through all of the religious, moral, legal, political, economic, and practical arguments—if the intimate adult relationship is over, then it's time to separate.

READER/CUSTOMER CARE SURVEY

We care about your opinions! Please take a moment to fill out our online Reader Survey at **http://survey.hcibooks.com**.

As a **"THANK YOU"** you will receive a **VALUABLE INSTANT COUPON** towards future book purchases as well as a **SPECIAL GIFT** available only online! Or, you may mail this card back to us.

(PLEASE PRINT IN ALL CAPS)

First Name _____ MI. _____ Last Name _____

Address _____ City _____

State _____ Zip _____ Email _____

1. Gender
- ❑ Female   ❑ Male

2. Age
- ❑ 8 or younger
- ❑ 9-12   ❑ 13-16
- ❑ 17-20   ❑ 21-30
- ❑ 31+

3. Did you receive this book as a gift?
- ❑ Yes   ❑ No

4. Annual Household Income
- ❑ under $25,000
- ❑ $25,000 - $34,999
- ❑ $35,000 - $49,999
- ❑ $50,000 - $74,999
- ❑ over $75,000

5. What are the ages of the children living in your house?
- ❑ 0 - 14   ❑ 15+

6. Marital Status
- ❑ Single
- ❑ Married
- ❑ Divorced
- ❑ Widowed

7. How did you find out about the book?
(please choose one)
- ❑ Recommendation
- ❑ Store Display
- ❑ Online
- ❑ Catalog/Mailing
- ❑ Interview/Review

8. Where do you usually buy books?
(please choose one)
- ❑ Bookstore
- ❑ Online
- ❑ Book Club/Mail Order
- ❑ Price Club (Sam's Club, Costco's, etc.)
- ❑ Retail Store (Target, Wal-Mart, etc.)

9. What subject do you enjoy reading about the most?
(please choose one)
- ❑ Parenting/Family
- ❑ Relationships
- ❑ Recovery/Addictions
- ❑ Health/Nutrition
- ❑ Christianity
- ❑ Spirituality/Inspiration
- ❑ Business Self-help
- ❑ Women's Issues
- ❑ Sports

10. What attracts you most to a book?
(please choose one)
- ❑ Title
- ❑ Cover Design
- ❑ Author
- ❑ Content

TAPE IN MIDDLE; DO NOT STAPLE

BUSINESS REPLY MAIL

FIRST-CLASS MAIL PERMIT NO 45 DEERFIELD BEACH, FL

POSTAGE WILL BE PAID BY ADDRESSEE

Health Communications, Inc.
3201 SW 15th Street
Deerfield Beach FL 33442-9875

FOLD HERE

Comments

If the intimate adult relationship is genuinely done, if the adult intimacy is dead and the caring and the respect that used to be there—or were supposed to be there and never were—is gone, then it's time to separate.

The idea of staying together for the kids is a cop out. It is simply and finally selfish.

There is no emotional benefit to a child who wakes up each morning, comes home from school each afternoon, and goes to sleep each night fearing that his caregivers may erupt in conflict yet again. If the intimate adult relationship has broken down to this point, staying together means that your kids live in a war zone. It means undermining the foundations of their confidence and shredding the safety net that might otherwise assure their security.

True, staying together may be easier. Resistance to change and the anxiety that arises when the future is unknown keeps many people living and working in destructive and abusive and unfulfilling situations.

True, separating is painful. Moving apart bursts everyone's bubble of denial. It makes public what the friends, neighbors, and extended family members already suspect but are so far too polite to talk about, or do so only in sympathetic (or even accusatory) whispers.

Most pointedly, separating may cause the kids increased distress because change is scary. But the arithmetic of the situation is compelling: stay together and expose your child for the remainder of his childhood to the stress and pain associated with a never-ending battle; or separate, help your child over the short-term stresses of transition, and then give him a chance to enjoy the remainder of his childhood in two separate but calm, loving, and supportive homes.

When Safety Is Compromised

Violent behavior must never be accepted in an intimate relationship. Tragically, millions of adults wake up to dangerous relationships every day. Domestic violence and spousal abuse are epidemic. You are far more likely to be assaulted by a family member or your intimate partner than by a stranger.

Chances are that you have a neighbor, coworker, friend, or family member who lives with domestic violence. You might suspect that something is different in their lives. You might even have tried to ask if everything is okay. It's not, but you're unlikely to hear about it. Shame, fear, denial, coercion, and misguided caring prompt empty reassurances that we are typically eager to accept. The reality of violence in intimate adult relationships is one of our society's best-kept secrets.

Why do otherwise intelligent and capable adults choose to remain in dangerous relationships?

Familiarity is a powerful incentive. Fear of the unknown is a powerful threat. Many adults tacitly re-create the abusive relationships they grew up with because they are familiar. They know their roles and their lines in this script. No matter the logic to the contrary, no matter the bruises and the broken bones, a familiar script can be more comfortable than walking on to the stage of an entirely new drama, even a healthier one.

Fear associated with threats is also a powerful motivator. Some adults remain in abusive intimate relationships in the belief that it is better to endure routine degradation and assault than to force a showdown with a partner who has threatened worse, such as destruction of property, theft of valuables, or even homicide or suicide.

A misplaced sense of nurturance can be part of the answer as well. One adult believes that he can rescue the other, even at the cost of his own well-being. He makes a commitment that enables his partner's destructive pathology or an excuse that ignores his own pain in the service of some higher goal, but the violence goes on, unabated.

Combine these factors with the depression and anxiety that can open the door to destructive adult relationships in the first place and that commonly grow out of them as well, and the result can cripple an individual's sense of worth and value. Angry and depressed, the partner's violence comes to feel deserved, like some cosmic penitence long overdue. Scared of the unfamiliar and terrified of the consequences of leaving, these adults go to sleep each night with no hope of any change.

Safety First!

Do you see yourself as living in danger?

Do you live with a violent partner?

Have you lashed out violently even once toward someone whom you love?

Take this opportunity to change. Renew your commitment never to tolerate violence of any kind. Discover better ways to cope with anger, to negotiate your differences, and to express your feelings. Reach out to a physician, therapist, or clergyperson right now. Open the phone book, find the name of the helpful professional that you scribbled down, and make a call.

Children who live with violent caregivers are more desperately

Safety First! *(continued)*

caught in the middle than all others. Not only does the experience of co-parental violence fail to teach children healthy means
of expressing feelings and resolving conflicts, it engenders crip-
pling guilt, anger, and fear. It can create indelible scripts that
prompt these children to re-create the relationships that their
parents lived, becoming adult victims and perpetrators of violence themselves.

Don't fool yourself: You can't hide it.

The kids know. They feel it. They read it in your face.

Do you think that tolerating your partner's abuse is somehow
protecting your children from the same? Think again: *We know
that the more frequently violence occurs between adults, the
more likely their child will also become a victim.*

As healthy partners, we must choose our own safety first and
foremost, never excusing violence in any form.

As healthy parents, we must teach our children never to tolerate violence in any form. We must give them healthy and
acceptable outlets for their feelings and effective means of protecting themselves when and if violence erupts.

As healthy co-parents, we must make the commitment never
to allow our differences to erupt into violence.

One act of violence is one too many. Don't pretend. Don't lie
to yourself or accept your partner's empty promises and fleeting
apologies as sufficient. You must act now to protect yourself
and your children.

Is Your Intimate Adult Relationship Child-Centered?

If the kids are your top priority, the decision to stay together or to break up with your intimate adult partner depends in part on how well this action serves the children's needs. Healthy adult relationships enrich their children's experience. Others trample it, causing the kids to feel like they're in the way, interfering with their parents' happiness or otherwise a burden.

This is not to say that you should stay together for the kids. Rather, as parents we must consider the impact of all of our decisions on our children.

Following is an informal and unscientific survey that can help you begin to think through how compatible your adult relationship and your responsibility to your kids really are. This survey cannot take the place of the advice of a mental health professional who knows you and your partner and your kids, but it can be a place to start.

To Complete This Survey

Fourteen simple statements follow. Each statement is worth 3 points.

If you believe that a given statement is generally true while your present intimate adult relationship remains intact, assign some or all of the points to the left-hand column.

If you believe that a given statement is generally true if your present intimate adult relationship were to end, assign some or all of the points to the right-hand column.

Points can be divided between the two columns in whole numbers (no fractions or decimals) as long as they sum to no more than three for each statement. Assigning more points (two or three out of three) to a column means that the statement is more likely true. Feel free to leave any item blank that you don't understand or about which you're not sure.

Stay together?	Example	Break up?
2	My child's shoes will fit better. (3)	1

In this example, the three points allotted to the statement, "My child's shoes will fit better," are split between the two columns. The answer suggests that the child's feet might be somewhat more comfortable if the adult relationship continues (two points) than if the adult relationships were to end (one point).

Sum the numbers in each column to compute a left-hand column "stay together" sum and a right-hand column "break up" sum.

The sum of the left column plus the sum of the right column cannot be more than forty-two.

Subtract the right-hand "Break up" column sum from the left-hand "Stay together" column sum to compute a decision index. For example, if the left-hand column sum is 30 and the right-hand column sum is 12, then the decision index is 30 – 12 or 18.

> [sum of left-hand "stay together" column] minus
> [sum of right-hand "break up" column] = decision index

Stay together?	Statement	Break up?
	My child's physical health will be better. (3)	
	My child will sleep better. (3)	
	My child will eat better. (3)	
	My child will be happier. (3)	
	My child will do better in school. (3)	
	I will feel better about myself as a parent. (3)	
	My child will get more one to one adult attention. (3)	
	My child's needs will be better fulfilled. (3)	
	My child will have a good role model. (3)	
	My child's schedule will be more predictable. (3)	
	My child's rules and consequences will be more consistent. (3)	
	My child's home will be happier. (3)	
	My child will have more friends. (3)	
	I will be happier. (3)	
Left column sum =	Sum the numbers that you assigned down each column. Enter the sum for each column at the bottom.	Right column sum =

The decision index will be forty-two if you assigned all values to the left-hand "stay together" column. It will be negative forty-two if you assigned all values to the right-hand "break up" column. A decision index of zero means that the two columns' sums are equal.

In general, a higher positive decision index approaching forty-two suggests that you believe that your adult relationship meets your children's needs. A lower decision index approaching negative forty-two suggests that you believe that the children's needs would be better served if the adult relationship were to end.

Finding Help and Enlisting Allies

Knowing when and how and whom to ask for help is among a mature adult's greatest strengths. Finding help when a conflict erupts in an intimate adult relationship can be the difference between living together and breaking up.

Finding help among friends, neighbors, and family can be a very stressful and challenging endeavor. Some of these people will come to your aid all too readily, driving the wedge that exists between you and your co-parent even deeper and risking exposing the kids to unnecessary and hurtful (although well-intentioned) information. Other friends and family will try to avoid being pulled into the conflict, feeling that they can't or won't take sides in a battle between people whom they care for. This may feel like a betrayal in the short run, but these people may end up in the long run becoming real emotional anchors for the kids.

Instead, it may be wise to seek out professional help.

Unfortunately, finding help when your relationship hurts can be much more difficult than finding help when your foot hurts (go to a podiatrist or orthopedist) or when you're experiencing emotional distress yourself (go to a psychotherapist). Most helping professionals are trained in the medical model of illness: diagnose the problem within the individual. This approach works for your foot pain because the problem is inside of you (a strained tendon) and may work for your emotional distress if the cause is internal (an explosive temper). This approach cannot work for a relationship issue because the problem does not exist within either individual; it exists between the individuals.

To Diagnose or Not to Diagnose?

Health insurance companies and managed-care corporations are typically among the most vocal and demanding proponents of the traditional medical model. Beware that when you or the professional you seek bills your third-party health carrier for payment, it is very likely that the service will be billed in one person's name and that that person will be diagnosed with a mental illness code from the *Diagnostic and Statistical Manual,* fourth edition (*DSM-IV*), published in 1994 by the American Psychiatric Association (with a text revision issued in 2000).

For example: when Adam and Eve's marriage began to suffer soon after their son's birth, the couple saw Dr. Brilliant for three sessions. Although both young parents were present, the doctor billed the couple's therapy under Adam's name with a corresponding diagnosis of adjustment disorder (DSM-IV code 309.9). Like most health-care providers, Dr. Brilliant never discussed these arcane codes and labels with Adam and Eve. He just wanted to get paid.

Lo and behold, at the divorce trial, Eve's unscrupulous attorney revealed the fact that Adam had been in psychotherapy and diagnosed with a mental illness. He argued on this basis that such a father should not become a young child's primary caregiver. Adam's attorney objected, to no avail. The health insurance records were clear.

Be a strong self-advocate. Above and beyond finding the right professionals to meet your needs, ask questions up front about labels, diagnoses, billing, and payment.

Consider what happens if you are concerned because your six-year-old has started wetting the bed. A visit to pediatrician will help determine whether there is a physical cause to the problem (a urinary tract infection, for example). If the child is physically healthy, the pediatrician might refer you to a cognitive-behavioral (child) therapist. This professional will help you to create "if . . . then contingencies" (rewards and punishments) that might give the child greater incentives to stay dry overnight.

But what if the bedwetting is the child's reaction to stress in the family? What if she only wets when Mom and Dad are arguing downstairs? Discovering this is the first hurdle. Responding to it requires the help of a professional who can work with the family system as a whole.

Clergy representing your faith may be willing and available to try to help, and indeed they may have a great deal to offer from a faith perspective. Above and beyond the particular religion's established position on matters like divorce, unmarried partnerships, children born out of wedlock, and gay marriage, it will be important to learn more about the particular clergyperson's background. Those with training and experience in individual, couples, or family counseling may be of greater assistance than those untrained but well-meaning others.

Couples, marital, and family therapists are mental health professionals who have training and experience responding to the "fit" among people. Regardless of whether they are addressed by the title "doctor" (and have the initials M.D., Ph.D., Psy.D., or Ed.D. following their name), these professionals are experts in understanding and helping relationships grow.

Couples, marital, and family therapies are feelings-oriented opportunities to improve the give-and-get balance within the relationship. The course of this work can be as unique as the parties involved, but will typically focus more on the process or the dynamics within the relationship than on the product or topic discussed. For example, conflicted co-parents who bring their disagreement about their daughter's bedtime to couples' therapy are more likely to work on how they express their respective positions than on the details of the child's bedtime. This can be an invaluable way to break down the barriers that can destroy relationships or, in some cases, to discover that those same barriers are insurmountable.

Mediation is the flip side of this coin. Mediation is one form of alternative dispute resolution (ADR). It is an opportunity to work with a professional who is specially trained (and in many states, licensed or certified) to help conflicted parties reach common ground on specific practical matters. A mediator might help conflicted co-parents settle the matter of a child's bedtime without ever addressing the couple's dynamics. Mediation is typically not an emotional, process-oriented intervention. Mediation is more likely to be explicitly focused on reaching child-centered conclusions about specific issues.

Arbitration is a fact-finding, decision-making process that is usually ordered by the court. An arbiter is a professional with specific training, certification, or licensure who is empowered to make a decision that is binding on the conflicted parties. An arbiter may be assigned or agreed upon in order to keep a matter out of court.

Guardian ad litem (GAL) is a professional appointed by the court to conduct an investigation for the purpose of providing the court with relevant facts, observations, and, in some cases, recommendations. When co-parents separate and contest their children's postseparation rights and responsibilities (custody), some courts ask for a specially trained, certified, or licensed GAL to investigate matters that may bear on the court's final recommendation. Although GALs and their roles and responsibilities differ widely across states, it may be important to choose a GAL with specialized training or expertise relevant to the matter under investigation. Some GALs are attorneys by training. Others are mental health professionals. Whether a GAL is a parent herself may also be a relevant consideration.

Parenting coordinators (PCs, known in some states as "special masters") are professionals appointed by the court to help conflicted co-parents settle many of their (postdivorce) differences outside of the courtroom. A PC is typically available on an as-needed basis to investigate, mediate, and, when necessary, arbitrate differences in child-centered matters within court-defined limits. Divorced parents who disagree about private versus public school enrollment, for example, may be able to bring the matter to their court-appointed PC in order to reach a conclusion.

The Lesson of Humpty Dumpty in One Sentence

*In the end, some things can't
be put back together even by all the king's horses
and all the king's men.*

Chapter 9

Scripting the Change

Words are incredibly powerful.

Words frame our experience and shape our reality. The words that we use to understand an event can determine whether an incident is remembered or forgotten, whether we experience trauma or trivia. Words can make the difference between whom we blame, whom we forgive, and how we see ourselves.

Psychology realized the power of words long ago. Researchers demonstrated, for example, that two adults witnessing the same event will report entirely different experiences depending upon how they are questioned about the event. "Did the green car hit the red car?" prompts most witnesses to respond yes or no when, in fact, no green car was involved at all.

Clinicians put the power of words to use in the form of cognitive-behavioral therapy (CBT). CBT helps a client to diminish his distress by changing the words he uses to understand his experience.

Words are especially powerful tools for shaping a child's experience. While adults often have a frame of reference within which to understand a new experience (memory of a prior experience, a friend's anecdote, or a story heard in the media), children may not. Without words to anchor understanding, children often become confused and distressed, falling back on a built-in need to blame themselves and on temperamental differences to act out or withdraw, to become sad or mad or scared.

As parents, we have the opportunity and the responsibility to help our children understand the world in which they live. Words are the tools we use to give our kids' experience meaning, and how we do this can shape the rest of their lives.

You can probably think of a hundred examples immediately. Here are two:

Your five-year-old hears a noise at night. If you explain how the wind makes the wooden house creak, she's reassured and falls asleep. If you were to suggest that wild beasts were trying to break through the walls, the night would be spent very differently.

Great Aunt Gertrude dies. If you explain that she's gone to sleep and she'll never wake up, your eight-year-old is likely to be scared to go to sleep for many nights to come. If you explain, instead, that Aunt Gertrude was very old and her body had reached its end (and her spirit is in heaven or all around us or will be reborn as a cow or . . .), then the child has a useful way to begin to understand loss and mortality.

So, what words do we use to explain the end of the adults' intimate relationship?

To Explain or Not to Explain, That Is the Question

Let's start by establishing that some explanation is necessary. To assume that kids won't notice or won't care that you and your partner no longer share the same bed or no longer speak, or that your relationship has ended or that your partner has moved out, is a mistake. The kids may not say anything. They might not ask any questions. They may even seem completely absorbed in the latest video game, but they notice and they wonder. Left unassisted, they will create their own less-than-accurate explanations.

Children are predisposed to blame themselves for their caregivers' behavior. They may not admit it, and if you ask, they will probably deny it fiercely, but the self-blame is there. It's deep down, and it's painful. The form that your child's self-blame takes might be built upon a distortion of a piece of the truth ("They got in a fight because of my grades") or upon a complete inaccuracy ("He left because I didn't like him"). Either way, left to fester, these uncorrected misbeliefs can become the seeds of later anger and depression and of fears that may undermine self and subsequent relationships.

"But my kids are too young to understand!"

No. The words have to be changed to suit the child's age and developmental abilities, language, and comprehension, but even a preverbal infant needs to have the story of her parents' break-up woven into the larger story of her life. She won't understand it while she's still two or three months old, but she still needs a script that explains the event that will be there, in the background, as she grows.

A script contains the words that we use to describe or manage a critical event in a child's life. It's a routine of words that helps our children to understand, to minimize self-blame and distorted perceptions. When scripts are developed to help kids cope with their parents' conflicts, they take on the additional and critical value of helping caregivers to keep their kids out of the middle by presenting a single, consistent message.

How Do We Create a Script?

In the best of all worlds, conflicted co-parents are able to put aside their differences to work together to see that all of their children's needs are met, including scripting critical life events.

Creating a script is simple. A script must be created now, while everyone is calm so that it's already there in your back pocket and ready to go when everyone's thinking is clouded by anger, fear, and sadness. If you can't work together unassisted to create a script, find someone to help you. Share this book with your helper so that everyone involved is working toward the same goals in the same ways.

A script must be suited to the child's abilities and needs, using words that are familiar to the child and keeping in mind that no one functions at their intellectual best under stress (a phenomenon known as regression). A script should probably be written at a level of understanding a bit less sophisticated than the child's show-off best, but it also needs to be able to grow with the child's understanding over time, gradually incorporating more sophisticated words and concepts.

How Do We Create a Script? *(contiunued)*

A script is truthful. With two necessary exceptions (see pages 105 and 114), there are few if any reasons to lie to your children. It's often easy to script an explanation based on a lie in the short term ("He's not dead; he's just away on a long trip"), but these lies will always cause more problems in the long run than they ever solve. If you believe that you cannot script an event without lying, a better approach may be to explain, "This isn't something that we can talk about until you're much older."

A script offers a benign explanation that defeats harmful explanations, which means assuring that the child is not blaming himself, that he's not blaming a caregiver in a way that interferes with a critical relationship, and that any unnecessary anger, sadness, or fear is diminished. This doesn't mean that the script resolves all the emotions associated with a critical event. Chances are that your kids will continue to feel whatever they feel about what happened, but their strong emotions will be given a benign focus.

A script keeps the child out of the middle. It's not enough for one parent to present one script and the other to present a second. We keep the kids out of the middle of our adult conflicts by presenting consistent messages that support the child and her ability to maintain a healthy relationship with each of her caregivers. Whether a script is written by one caregiver alone or by the co-parents jointly, it needs to be presented consistently by all caregivers.

Scripting a Conflict

What do we say to our kids when they walk into the middle of an argument? Or when we discover them perched at the top of the stairs, pretending to be asleep, or listening in on the phone extension during a heated exchange?

Ignoring it won't make it go away. Words like, "Nothing happened here!" and "You didn't see that!" fuel denial and confusion and turn important subjects into forbidden objects. You need to say something to give your kids some framework within which they might begin to understand what they just witnessed or overheard.

Taking your feelings out on them will only compound the problem. They're probably already scared and confused. Exposing your kids to your anger ("I told you to go to bed!"), your grief ("It's all over!"), your fear ("How will we manage without her?"), or your needs ("I'm all alone now, Billy. Come give me a hug . . .") risks burying the child's feelings and needs under your own and puts them in the middle of something they can't possibly understand.

But diving in prematurely with a canned script won't work either. A script needs to be there for the child when he needs it, not for you when you're at a loss.

Start here, and every time you're uncertain how to proceed, assess the child's needs and beliefs. Where is the child at? For example, the six-year-old who gets off the school bus, sits at the table to eat his snack, and casually says, "What's sex?" probably isn't ready for a factual lesson about intercourse and procreation. Start, instead, by assessing what the child needs: "What do you think?" If the answer is, "Sam told me that it's a fruit," then you're likely to proceed quite differently than if the answer is, "Some big kids were talking about private parts."

When you discover that the same child just witnessed his two beloved caregivers yelling at one another, follow his lead. Respond to his posture and his expression—"You look pretty scared"—or try to get at what he's thinking—"What do you think that was all about?" At worst, you'll get the all-purpose empty answers, "Nothing," or "I don't know," or even an angry, "I don't care." To these you can at least make certain that you leave the door open for later: "Okay, but you know that you can talk to me or Daddy any time you want, right?"

Did you notice the "me or Daddy" part of that response? In that subtle and common phrase, you've communicated that even though the adults are at odds, the safety net is still intact. We're both there for you.

What about when your effort to determine where the child is at yields a real answer?

If you ask, "What do you think that was all about?" and the reply is, "Daddy hates you," then you have an opening to use your script:

"Seems that way, huh? Well, we don't hate each other, but sometimes we get pretty mad at each other. We're trying to learn how to be mad less often and more quietly. We're real sorry that you had to hear this."

One word of warning: It may be tempting here to offer short-term reassurance in the form of promises that you can't keep, like "we'll always stay together." Don't.

Scripting the Separation

When co-parents plan to separate, a script prepared and presented in advance will help the child be ready for what may be a very emotional change.

How long in advance of a planned separation should the child be told? The answer depends both on the child's age and on practical realities that are unique to the child's situation. A younger child with developmentally less sophisticated means of coping should be given less lead time. An older child might do better with more. As a general rule of thumb, a child should be given no more advance warning than a number of days equal to twice his age in years. Thus, at the outside, a four-year-old might be told that Daddy is moving out eight days ahead of the event. A ten-year-old might be given as many as twenty days' notice.

Beware here, as always, that general rules offer at best weak guidelines. The situation needs to be addressed to suit the unique details of your child's world, including whether and how the child will be aware that Dad is packing his things and real calendar activities. The teenager preparing for final exams, for example, might be told about an impending separation just before the event so as not to interfere with his studying. Birthdays, holidays, and vacations may similarly bear on when the separation is planned to occur and how long in advance a child is notified.

A script explaining an adult separation should make the child's world as predictable as possible. It should answer each of the child's reasonably self-centered concerns first and foremost:

1. "Where will I be?" (Where will I sleep? Eat? Get the bus?)
2. "When will I see you?" (When will I be at Dad's? At Mom's?)
3. "How long will you be apart?" (When will you get back together?)

Listen carefully to your child's questions and needs. A child faced for the first time with the news of his parents' separation often becomes very concerned about something that you may see as unimportant or trivial. Questions like, "But where will Rover be?" and "Can I still go to swim practice?" are clues to the child's critical emotional anchors—those possessions, relationships, and activities that are important to his sense of security. Discovering that a pet or a particular pillow, for example, are important to your child may be reason enough to agree, "Of course your pillow can go to Mommy's new house with you."

One Sample Script About Separation

When they first decided to divorce, Mark and Joanne met briefly with a local child psychologist, Dr. Brilliant. This consultation was useful in at least one way. The psychologist helped the couple to agree to a script they could use to explain the separation to their son, Frankie, even though he was just a toddler at the time. Over time, this script has evolved to suit the child's growing maturity, but it has always assured that Frankie has heard a similar explanation from his mom (who has since shared it with her new husband, John) and from his dad across the years. In this one simple way, the co-parents have kept Frankie out of the middle.

The script goes like this:

"Once upon a time there was a man named Mark and a woman named Joanne. They met and fell in love and got married and made you. Mark loved Joanne, and Joanne loved Mark, and they both loved you.

"The love between adults can break, and ours has," the parent explains. "But the love between a parent and a child cannot break. Ours never will. Your mom loves you very much, and your dad loves you very much, even though Mom and Dad no longer love each other.

"Now we have two homes, and we each have new adult loves. That means that you have two homes and twice as much love."

Create a Future Album

In the same way that some parents create photo albums documenting the child's important developmental milestones (first steps, first day of school, first tooth lost), you can create a future album for your children.

A future album is a collection of notes, ideas, and full-fledged letters that you write to your child now, to record and explain the events of her life, but which you intend for her to read sometime in the future. You might write to your two-year-old as you imagine her at twenty-five, helping her to understand the events that are impacting her now even though she may not receive the letter for another twenty-three years.

"Dear Maggie," you write. "You're just a toddler as I write, but I want to help you understand why your father and I . . ."

For some parents, creating a future album is insurance against the possibility that you'll forget or not be around to answer her questions when she's old enough to understand the answers. For other parents, locked out of a child's life by court order, by distance, or by choice, a future album can be a gift that might someday begin to bridge that chasm.

(Re-)Defining Family

At issue is whether and how to communicate that, after the co-parents separate, the child continues to have one family (albeit living apart) or begins to have two separate families. This one is controversial for conflicted co-parents and for the professionals who seek to assist them alike.

In favor of the "one-family-apart" argument is the likelihood that the family group will be together in the future despite the separation, as when Mom and Dad (and their new intimate partners) attend Billy's concert or Sally's graduation. This argument suggests that the child will find it emotionally easier at these events to conceive of the group in the singular: "My family is here."

The argument in favor of the two-family conceptualization is based upon the child's need for structure in the form of boundaries, predictability, and consistency. From this perspective, once the intimate adult relationship dissolves (regardless of marital status) and especially once the caregivers establish separate homes, the script should describe the child as belonging to two separate families. Yes, those families may converge at common events, but no, Mom and Dad will not be getting back together.

The two-family script is particularly useful when separated co-parents have very different expectations and consequences (that is, when consistency is poor). Conceptualizing the two families as distinct and separate helps to make the differences between the two homes more easily understood. With this explanation in place, the answer to, "But Dad lets me. . . ." is simply, "Those are the rules in that house. The rules in this house are different."

It may be that co-parents who are more cooperative, who communicate better, and who are better able to put their children's needs first, before their own, can make the one-family-apart script work. Under these very civil and child-centered conditions, the kids are presumably less distraught, and there is less need for the reassurance of firm and clear boundaries.

In the interest of keeping kids out of the middle, start by trying out a two-family script that goes something like this:

"Once upon a time, we made one family together with three members: You and your mother and me. Since your mother and I stopped loving each other and moved apart, we've become two families. One family is made up of you and your mother (and her new boyfriend). The other family is made up of you and me (and Doris, your stepmom). You belong to two families."

For some children, a little bit of rationalization adds a nice coda: "You're pretty lucky, you know. Having two families means that you have two bedrooms and get two birthdays and two times as many holidays!"

Scripting the Transitions Between Homes

When the conflict between adults persists well beyond the end of the intimate relationship and the physical separation, the kids are vulnerable to being caught in the crossfire any time the adults come together. The parents come together most often when the child transitions between their care.

Transitioning Through School

Transitioning through school (or daycare or camp) might offer one practical solution. In one such plan, Mom ends her parenting responsibilities (physical custody) when she drops Billy at school on Monday morning, and Dad begins his parenting responsibilities (becomes the POD) when he picks Billy up on Monday after school. Although this plan creates dilemmas about who is responsible if Billy gets hurt on the playground at lunch on Monday and what to do with his belongings (very few children want to drag a suitcase to school with them, and few school offices are willing to regularly provide storage for their students' belongings), it can help to minimize the adults' face-to-face encounters and the opportunity for renewed conflict.

Transitioning Through the Child's Therapy Appointment

In some situations, a child's psychotherapy appointment can become a very constructive time and place to transition between caregivers. Here's how:

When a child's parents are conflicted, that child is at high risk for emotional and behavioral difficulties. Enrolling that child in psychotherapy can be a very sound choice, at least in order to give the child a port in the storm. Ideally, all caregivers will be involved in establishing this therapy from the start and will remain supportive and responsive as the therapy continues.

With the therapist's agreement, a child's appointments can be scheduled on a day and at a time that allows the sending parent to deliver the child to the appointment, check in with the therapist and then leave, and the receiving parent to arrive at the end of the hour, check in with the therapist, and take the child for the start of her parenting time.

Better still, some therapists will agree to extend the appointment from one hour to one and a half hours, splitting the additional thirty minutes to allow a fifteen-minute consultation time with each parent at either end of the child's therapy hour. The purpose here is not to enlist the child's therapist as the co-parents' go-between, but to help the co-parents stay involved, keep the therapist up to date, and tacitly communicate to the child that the parents at least agree on the therapy, if little else.

Transitioning in Public

When transitioning through school isn't practical because the child isn't enrolled, because the parenting schedule doesn't coincide with the school schedule, or because of other practical considerations, transitioning in a public place may be the second-best option. All but the most enraged adults behave more civilly when other people are watching. The town library, a grocery store parking lot halfway between the homes, or the local police station are common choices, but beware of what the location means to the children. The police station, for example, can suggest that one or both of the parents—or the child himself!—are somehow bad or in trouble.

When conflicted caregivers must meet face-to-face to transition a child, scripting the interaction for the adults is sometimes necessary. This script, like those described earlier, seeks to decrease anxiety and the opportunity for conflict by making behavior predictable.

In this script, the lines are simple and the roles are clear. The face-to-face transition is not the time or place to discuss schedules, exchange money, or bring up anything of any substance. Even updates about the child's well-being are delivered in writing from one adult hand to the other adult's hand (never making the child into the courier) or, better still, by voice message or e-mail at another time.

The sending parent arrives with the child and greets the receiving parent pleasantly and without unspoken tension: "Hi, Adam. How are you?"

The receiving parent makes eye contact with his co-parent and calmly says, "Hi, Jane. Fine, thanks," (this is one of the two times when a lie is acceptable and expected see page 95) and then turns to the child with a wide smile, "Hey, Junior! Give me five, buddy!"

The sending parent turns to the child and (handing him his stuff) says, "See you later, Junior" (kiss, hug). "Have a great time with your dad!"

The receiving parent prompts the child, "Say good-bye to your mom!"

The sending parent drives away first, leaving the receiving parent to pack up the child and leave at his leisure.

These several illustrations—scripts for adult separation, conflict, and the transition between homes—are just the beginning. When you and your co-parent script an event in your child's life, you are working together to assure that some of the holes in his safety net are woven tight. You are creating just a bit more consistency and, in so doing, you're freeing him to devote his energies to playing and learning and exploring rather than worrying and wondering about his world.

What other events might you and your co-parent work together to script? The list is as endless as your child's life is unique. A few examples might be the introduction of a new adult partner, a parent's plan to relocate to a new home or a new city, a loved one's illness, injury, or death, even the co-parents' reunion. By anticipating the event and the child's needs with a simple and consistent script, you and your co-parents are cooperating to keep him out of the middle.

Chapter 10

How to Answer the Kids' Concerns:
The Power of "We"

I f you and your co-parent can only agree to do one thing to support your kids while you navigate the course of your intimate adult relationship, do this: speak in the first-person plural—the royal "we":

"We have decided that you can . . ."

"We are concerned that you . . ."

"We've talked about what happened and . . ."

This one simple imperative, as much as any therapy, intervention, or support, will reassure your kids that the safety net is intact—that the co-parenting team is still there, behind the scenes, taking care of them no matter what else may be happening in the family. "We" communicates that the foundation is sound even if the roof has blown off and the walls of self are sagging.

"We" messages reveal that the co-parents are still a team. "We" means consistency and collaboration, the bedrock of healthy co-parenting.

"We" messages communicate that you and your co-parent are working together to meet the kids' needs.

"We" messages minimize the child's opportunity for blame and splitting, the natural tendency to polarize parenting differences into good versus bad, white versus black. (Read more about children's expectations in Chapter 14, and about splitting in Chapter 13.)

And "we" messages help to keep the kids out of the middle.

Of course, in order to be able to speak in terms of "we," you and your co-parent must be able to put aside your differences, communicate, cooperate, and compromise. "We" messages require that you are able to maintain enough mutual respect and trust to reach an agreement and keep it, to follow through with a promise, and to stand firm behind a parenting decision that may not be your first choice but which is, in fact, the result of your mutual collaboration.

Here's your chance to practice. The following six statements are among the most common that conflicted and separated co-parents hear from their kids. Think through how you would (and how you should) respond to each before reading on. Your answers will be graded on an A, B, C, D, or F scale.

"Why Are You and Daddy Living Apart?"

This is the bottom-line "why?" lingering there in your kids' thinking regardless of their age or how obvious and familiar the answer might be or how long ago the conflict and separation occurred. It is precisely the same sort of "why?" that runs circles through the thoughts of the bereaved long after a loved one has died. In both instances—coping

with the parents' separation and coping with the death of a loved one—
"why?" is about struggling for emotional acceptance. It is seldom a
request for more facts.

"Your father is a #@$%! So we got out."

Do you hear that loud, bleating noise in the background signaling
failure? Wrong answer, but thanks for playing. Try again later.

Even if her father is, in fact, worthy of that expletive, telling her so
serves your needs, not hers. Your response is likely to contaminate her
relationship with her father, and it may needlessly complicate her relationship with you as she recognizes that loving one parent is a betrayal
of the other.

"We've talked about this a hundred times, sweetie. Can't you let it
go?" This reply is marginally better because no damage has been done
to the child's relationship with her other parent, but otherwise it misses
the boat completely. Almost as bad, it says that the parent speaking is
emotionally unavailable (on this subject at least) and closes the door
on future discussion of this subject. Give yourself a solid D.

Of course you're allowed to become overwhelmed. Of course there
are times and places that are better or worse for deep and emotional
talks. Better would be, "It's been a long day, honey. Ask me again tomorrow, and we'll figure this out some more, okay?" This is a D+ or C–
response.

"Remember what we've talked about? Your daddy and I grew apart.
We stopped loving each other." Two points for answering with a "we"
statement. Two more points for not blaming anyone. Give yourself half
credit if, indeed, you've offered the same, consistent, and predictable
response time after time, and another half point for your patience

despite what sounds like a repetitive question ("Tell me again, Mommy!"). This is a C response. A passing grade.

Preface that reply with a kind and empathic, "What do you think?" or even a curious and child-centered, "What got you thinking about that again?" and your grade moves up to B. Good job. Of course, this preface might take you in an entirely different direction ("Because I want to split up with my boyfriend" or "Because Sammy's parents are always fighting like you and Daddy used to . . .") that requires flexibility and patience on your part. Chances are, however, that "What do you think?" will lead you more or less directly back to a lingering wish for reunion.

The A answer? "What do you think?" opening the door to "We stopped loving each other," followed up with reassurance: "But your daddy will always love you, and I will always love you, no matter what."

"It's My Fault That You Broke Up!"

This isn't a question, but it still demands a reply.

The easy and obvious answer is, "Of course not, sweetie. You had nothing to do with it." Give yourself a C for this response so far. You can improve your grade by responding carefully to the necessary follow-up, "Well, then whose fault is it?"

Red alert. Think first. This is much harder than it seems.

"It's your mom's fault." Oops. Give yourself an F. Even if that is somehow factually true, the person whom you're talking about is still his other parent. Your anger has no place here. It serves your needs—not your kids'—to place the blame this way.

"It's all my fault. I should have . . ." Give yourself a D. Martyrdom is not to be rewarded. Nothing's gained by laying your guilt on your child's shoulders. This is an adult feeling that belongs in an adult discussion and nowhere else.

"It's no one's fault, honey. It's just the way things turned out." Maintain your C. Very average. This shallow reassurance provides no information and probably leaves the child wondering. The good news is that he'll ask again later, and you'll get to try again.

"It's both of our faults, buddy—your mom and I. We both made mistakes." Better. Give yourself a B, maybe even a B+. You offered an answer using "we" without blaming anyone.

Give yourself an A if you first ask, "What do you really think?" Only then, after you understand more fully what really prompted the question ("Mommy said it was my fault!" or "My teacher said that divorce is wrong!" or even more likely, "I just want you guys back together!") can you decide if "It's both of our faults, buddy—your mom and I. We both made mistakes," is still the best answer.

And for extra credit?

You were on your game when you asked "What do you really think?" first. This prompted him to break down and reply, "I just want you guys back together!" This response reveals that his real interest isn't about blame so much as it is about reunion.

So, how do you best reply to that?

"When Will We Get Back Together Again?"

In fact, most children who have any memory of their parents living together—even if that memory is colored by conflict—maintain at least a faint and irrational hope for reunion. Our media glorifies and roman-ticizes this hope, sometimes communicating that children can engineer their parents' reunion against all odds, as in the popular Disney movie *The Parent Trap.* (Erich Kästner's book, produced by Disney as a movie in 1961 and remade in 1998, with one sequel in 1986 and two more in 1989, speaks to the popularity of this hope.)

How do you respond when your child asks, eyes wide and tearful, "When will we get back together again?"

"Some day, sweetie, when your dad gets his act together."

No and no. Give yourself a D at best. The uncertainty that lingers when a reunion *could* happen some day will eat away at everyone's security, making each new day that the reunion doesn't occur a disap-pointment. Add to this the blame and splitting (even if it's warranted) in making Dad a bad guy, and this answer is a double whammy that probably does more harm than good.

"Your dad and I are working on that." Marginally better. Maybe a low C. This is a "we" statement (even though the word is only implied), but that open-endedness lingers there and invites most kids to repeat, "But when?" with growing desperation.

Tack on a "What do you think, sweetie?" before either of these prior responses, and you can improve your grade a full letter. Chances are that "What do you think?" in this instance will elicit hopes more than expectations. "Tomorrow" or "next week" are among the child's expectable responses, opening the door for you to first validate the feelings, "I know you really hope for that," before anything else.

Score a solid B or better by following up your empathic and support-ive, "What do you think?" with "Remember what we told you, buddy?

We won't know before August 1" (in the case, for example, of a trial separation). Rather than leave the kids hanging one day to the next indefinitely, wondering when the "temporary" separation will end and how the healing is going, the better alternative is to declare a decision-making time frame: "We're moving apart. We're going to work hard to figure out what to do next. We won't know anything before August 1. On August 1, we'll either decide to get back together, to stay apart permanently, or that we need another three months to keep working at it."

The response that earns an A follows up your "What do you think?" query with a clear and compassionate statement of reality that helps the child to move on. Speaking quietly, offering physical reassurance when it's accepted (a held hand, a hug), the best answer allows the child to grieve: "We're not getting back together, honey. The love between Daddy and me has broken and can't be fixed, but the love between you and Daddy and between you and me can never break."

"Never, Mommy?"

"Not ever, sweetie."

"Do You Still Love My Mommy?"

Red alert! This question looks like it was clipped from a Hallmark card complete with a puppy dog photo, but it can be a minefield full of trouble. Think carefully before you take your first step forward.

"Yes. Of course."

"I'll always love your mom."

"I love her like a friend."

"I love all of God's children."

Give yourself a D at best for any of these responses.

"But it's the truth!" you object. "I do still love her. I never wanted to break up!"

This is among the most difficult emotional circumstances an adult can face: when a love relationship ends unilaterally, despite your continuing commitment and contrary to all of your deepest desires. This situation reasonably stirs up a storm of powerful emotions, from a desperate, pleading longing to near-crippling feelings of inadequacy and loss, to a raging sense of betrayal. Any or all of these are reason enough to find a helper with whom you can try to find some peace.

Even if this is the truth, your kids need closure. All but the most mature among them will hear your professions of undying love (even if you try to disguise it as platonic or religious) and become confused and caught in the middle.

The message in expressing your undying love for your former intimate partner and continuing co-parent is that she's the bad guy. If you still love her, then why are you apart? You were jilted. This message simultaneously fuels your kids' natural and expectable wish for reunion and damns their other parent. This well-intentioned and truthful reply might interfere with your child's ability to love her other parent, to grieve and move on, and to ever accept either of her parents' new partners.

Chapter 9 cautioned that, as parents, we must never lie to our kids except in two necessary situations. The first occurs when conflicted co-parents are face-to-face using a previously established script to manage the interaction. This is the second:

"No, sweetie. I don't love your mommy anymore." This is the C response. Truthful or not, as long as your obvious feelings, behavior, and the words that she overhears when she listens in on the phone extension or reads when she peeks at your e-mail don't suggest otherwise, this response closes a painful door. It will help her to grieve what is lost and begin to move on.

Start with "What do you think?" and change your grade to a B. In this instance, your empathic, child-centered preface may reveal a great deal that will direct how you should respond and may even highlight issues that you and your co-parent need to address.

"Daddy, do you still love my mommy?"

"What do you think, darling?"

"I need to know because Mommy told me that she still loves you."

This calls for an empathic, "Hmmm. That must be confusing" and a conference with your co-parent as soon as possible: why is she putting your kids in the middle this way?

"You do still love Mommy because I heard you and Mr. Smith talking." Embarrassed? Angry? Don't scold. There's much more here than a little curious eavesdropping. Try, "Boy, it's hard to understand when you hear little bits and pieces of someone else's conversation. But I'm glad that you asked . . . ," followed by clarification as best as possible and a renewed commitment to only cry on your friends' shoulders behind closed doors in the future.

"I hope not, because Mommy's got a new boyfriend." Oh . . . your best mature coping skills now kick in. Take a deep breath. Remain child-centered. Respond to her needs now and your needs (cry? yell? celebrate? call your attorney?) later. Your daughter is probably asking for help to cope with this news. She may be looking for your approval to care about this new adult in her life. Start with, "Well, how do you feel about that?" and go slowly. The minefield just became more dangerous.

If "What do you think?" doesn't redirect the conversation entirely, then the A response to, "Do you still love Mommy?" is a reassuring "we" statement: "No, sweetie. Our adult love broke. It's done. But Mommy always loves you, and I always love you, no matter what."

"I Don't Have to Listen to Him! He's Not My Parent!"

Out of the frying pan and into the fire.

This rant highlights a dozen different issues including the child's hope for reunion (*If I aggravate Mom's new boyfriend, then he'll leave, and she'll get back together with Dad!*), the biology and legalities that define parenthood (a theme that adoptive parents inevitably face at some point along the way), the autonomy-building defiance that characterizes adolescence, the torn alliances that often grow in the fertile soil of co-parental conflict, and simple, frank, and uncomplicated rage.

"You're right. He's not your parent. You only have to do what I say!" Grade yourself an F–. Worse than missing the mark, worse even than expressing your selfish anger at the new caregiver who has come on the scene, this response fuels your child's anger, validates his defiance, and digs the hole that he's found himself in—caught in the middle— even deeper. This response empowers your child as your ally, contaminates his relationship with other caregivers, and simply hurts him.

Go to the principal's office. You're on detention.

Avoid detention with a D– grade by responding, "You're right. He's not your parent. You only have to do what your mother and I say!" This may be a legally valid observation to the extent that this new caregiver has no authority to direct your child's behavior, but when did your child get her law degree? This response is marginally better only because it contains a subtle suggestion of a "we" statement in the phrase "your mother and I."

"What do you think?" doesn't belong here. She said what she thinks. She didn't ask a question.

Are you tempted to ask, "What did he tell you to do?" The worries that prompt this question might be reasonable, but beware that you risk stepping over an important boundary by implicitly asking your child to report on activities in the other home. Unless you have immediate safety concerns, best not to ask this question now. Later, out of range of little ears, perhaps you can alert your co-parent that there's dissent afoot and even ask what role her new partner is playing in the home. If he is, indeed, sharing parenting responsibilities there, you may have a new co-parent.

"He's your mother's boyfriend, sweetie. If your mother says so, then I'm afraid that you do have to do what he says." Give yourself a weak C. On the positive side, you didn't undermine the new caregiver's authority. On the negative side, you expressed it as a regret suggesting that you agree: life shouldn't be this way.

"He's your mother's boyfriend, sweetie. I've met him, and your mother loves him. We're all working together as co-parents now." Okay. Better. Give yourself a B. Good job creating an expanded sense of "we."

Preface this statement with something that acknowledges the strong emotions being expressed without tacitly agreeing with them, and you're headed to the front of the class. The A response starts with, "Wow, you're really mad about this!" or "It's really hard keeping up with all of these changes, isn't it?" followed by, "But you do need to do what he says. We're all working together as co-parents now."

"Can I Sleep Over at Dad's Instead?" The Dilemma of the Disneyland Co-Parent

Responding to this question is almost as hard as responding to the angry child who announces, "I'm out of here. I'm going to Dad's!" These sentiments test a caregiver's maturity and the strength of the safety net the co-parents are supposed be weaving together. Both call for co-parenting communication, cooperation, and consistency worthy of an Olympic sporting team. How to respond to a child's requests and demands is discussed further in Chapter 11.

Healthy parents know and gradually come to accept that parenting success means letting your child go and allowing her to build autonomy. When you feel forced to let go prematurely, however, anger, resentment, and our worst parenting fears erupt: "I'm a horrible parent! She hates me!" "I'm not good enough!" "She loves her other parent more!" "I'm going to lose her forever."

These fears of loss and inadequacy (often exaggerated by misdirected animosity toward a former intimate partner) can prompt an immature and needy caregiver to try to win a child's time, love, and attention the same way that a businessperson might try to win a lucrative contract. The deal is sweetened with enticements, perks, and ever more exciting fun. Undeserved and unexpected gifts appear and opportunities abound, often heedless of very real and very obvious budgetary, scheduling, and even health and safety concerns. Parenting structures go out the window. This parent, sometimes generically known as the "Disneyland Dad," runs a selfish, shortsighted, and unwinnable race to pull the child closer.

This is a recipe for disaster. The Disneyland Dad corrupts his kids' emotional security. He clearly values happiness more than health. His kids, given too much discretion, naturally want to be with the parent who is more fun and less demanding. This is a recipe for becoming adultified or infantilized at least, and growing up terribly insecure, self-centered, angry, or depressed at worst.

The healthy parent faced with a Disneyland co-parent only has three choices.

The healthy choice, of course, is to bring the concern directly to the other adult in an effort to reach a new agreement on the structures with which you will together weave the child's safety net. If direct dialogue fails, this concern is dangerous enough to warrant seeking out professional assistance in the interest of the same goals.

Unfortunately, too many adults choose instead to grab the child's other arm and play tug-of-war, lowering expectations and offering bigger and bigger incentives, back and forth, the way that neighboring gas stations used to conduct price wars, dropping their costs and giving away ever more enticing goodies in a constant effort to win the next customer.

And then there are those adults who choose a third option. Believing that her co-parent is being too indulgent, her parenting becomes more rigid. She thinks that she can compensate for her co-parent's selfish and destructive choices. This well-intentioned effort is doomed to failure, however, as the co-parents gradually become more polarized, sometimes causing a tragic and unnecessary break between the child and the parent who is trying to reinforce the structure in her life that takes the form of transition resistance or refusal.

So what is the best response when a child asks, "Can I sleep over at Dad's instead?"

It's not: "No! You may not. This is my time, and you're not going anywhere!"

This response earns you a generous D. The authoritarian tone with no hint of empathy is likely to elicit an immediate angry reply in the form of defiance ("I'm going anyway! I don't care what you say!") or delayed anger, in a variety of indirect forms. Even worse, this response selfishly and inaccurately suggests that the time (and, by extension, the child) belongs to you, when neither does.

Only the fact that this response sets a firm limit, however poorly expressed, prevents it from failing entirely.

An average, C-level response to a child's request reinforces that the co-parents work together as a team using a "we" statement: "I'll talk to your dad, and we'll let you know." Make that a C+ by reducing anxiety with specifics: "And we'll let you know by supper."

Preface this reply with a nonthreatening, shrug-of-the-shoulders question about the feelings or plans that motivate the request, and move up to a B. For example, "What's up, buddy? Got some plans?"

Be careful here. It's easy to slide down the slippery slope back to an F. If your question carries any hint of anger, loneliness, or neediness, any suggestion that you are trying to look behind your former partner's closed doors, you're putting the child in the middle all over again. Anything that prompts a child to feel that he has to take care of you rather than vice versa will mean you have failed this course.

The A+ response incorporates three elements: "What's up, buddy? Got some plans?"; then, depending on the response, "Okay, I'll talk to your dad, and we'll let you know by supper"; and a prompt and definitive follow-up, after conferring with your co-parent in the form of either, "We've talked about it, and he'll be here at five" or "We've talked about it, and we can't make it work this time. Sorry."

Can Some Children Choose?

There is a reasonable argument to be made in favor of giving some children under some circumstances the discretion to choose between their homes. In fact, although state laws bearing on custodial discretion in the context of divorce vary widely, many states recognize the value of considering the preferences of a "mature minor."

What exactly is a mature minor, and how is this developmental threshold measured? No one yet knows.

For our purposes, perhaps the following guidelines can be useful.

A child's expressed wish to shift to his other parent's care should always be acknowledged but will only be granted when:

Can Some Children Choose? *(continued)*

1. The child's wish is not obviously intended to escape what he perceives to be a burden in one home (a punishment, a chore, a sibling conflict, an undesirable limit or responsibility, for example).
2. The child is intellectually and emotionally mature enough to understand the consequences of the wish, including when he will return to the home that he has asked to leave.
3. The child's wish is expressed no less than twenty-four hours in advance of the desired change.
4. The co-parents are able to discuss and agree to the change first, before either offers an opinion to the child. Should the timing prove inadequate (because one or both co-parents are unavailable, for example) or the co-parenting dialogue otherwise fails, the default response to the child will be, "Sorry. We can't work that out."
5. One co-parent's choice to deny the request is sufficient for the request to be refused.

The co-parents' mutual decision to grant or deny the wish is expressed to the child by all co-parents in the form of a "we" statement: "We've worked it out. Mom will pick you up," or "We can't make this work."

Chapter 11

Creating a Child-Centered Parenting Plan:

Whose Time Is It Anyway?

A n unfortunate reality is that conflicted co-parents commonly dispute the division of their children's time in the same way that they contest the division of their savings and the possession of their furniture. Hours to be spent with Johnny are calculated down to the minute and assigned different value depending on whether the child is expected to be awake or asleep, in school or at band practice, or available for interaction. How long a child will be in one parent's care as opposed to the other parent's care becomes a ratio to be counterbalanced and bartered against assets and child-support dollars.

The fact that much of this self-centered and picayune process is sanctioned by (and even mandated by) the law is a vestige of our history as a chauvinistic, industrialized culture. Any process that looks at the child as one or both of the parents' property and proceeds to divide the child's time like so much pizza to be sliced and shared among hungry teenagers is wrong, obsolete, antique, and even harmful.

Ask yourself: Who has more to give, the child or the parent? Should the child's very limited resources be divided so as to benefit the parents, or should, instead, the parents' combined resources be divided so as to benefit the child?

To treat the child's time like a commodity to be apportioned suggests to everyone, including the child herself, that the parents are needy, and the child is responsible for fulfilling that need. Any healthy, child-centered parent or professional recognizes this as an unhealthy role reversal.

In fact, the child is the one in need. The adults have the opportunity and responsibility to see that the child's needs are fulfilled, which means both the privilege and the burden of assuring that the broccoli is eaten and deciding when the training wheels come off and which movies she can watch and waiting endlessly for her next appointment, lesson, practice, rehearsal, date, or nap to end.

A child-centered parenting plan is never concerned with a parent's complaint that he is "missing out." A parent who argues that the number of hours he's been allotted is "not fair" is being selfish. As adults, we are responsible to get our needs met through other adults, not from our kids. To expect that the child will be present (and awake and otherwise unoccupied) to meet these needs threatens to adultify or infantilize the child.

The History of Custody Assignments

The word "custody" says it all: ownership, possession, and territoriality.

Under English common law, children and wives were once considered to be the father/husband's property, like so many chickens or bags of flour. The man, as "lord of the manor," was free to do with his possessions as he chose, largely ungoverned by any law. Children—especially boys—had value as free labor on the American frontier and on the farm; by the early 1800s, children were working sixteen-hour shifts in soot-caked factories as the Industrial Revolution took over the economy.

In those days, children were owned as "chattel." Custody did, indeed, mean ownership. A man who had reason to leave his wife kept the kids as his possessions. Period. The mother had no stake in the children once delivered and no claim to custody of any kind.

As early as the mid-1800s, British courts began to acknowledge that the mother-child bond had value. Even so, it was another 100 years before courts in the United Kingdom and even later in the United States began to adopt this tenet in the form of the Tender Years Doctrine.

The Tender Years Doctrine declares the vulnerability of children and the mother's unique capacity for nurturance. Laws enacted on this basis established that when parents separate, children under the age of thirteen (or sixteen, in some instances) were to remain in their mother's care, all other things being equal. Although most Tender Years presumptions have since been taken off the books, a basic belief in women's superiority as parents persists into the present, even among family law judges, even when the law specifically prohibits it.

By the end of the last century, courts began to consider that any one-size-fits-all custodial determination inevitably fails to recognize the unique needs of the individuals they sought to serve. The resulting emphasis on each child as an individual is consistent with most people's contemporary values, even though the resulting need for individually tailored determinations has dramatically overburdened most family law courtrooms. In response, a series of postseparation care theories have arisen.

The Least Detrimental Alternative (1979) established that, while we may not know what's best for our children, we can often agree on what is worst. Under this guideline, a child's postseparation care is to be assigned so as to minimize the harm that the child will endure.

The Psychological Parent Rule (1995) established that children should be placed exclusively in the care of the preseparation primary caregiver.

The Approximation Rule (2002) recommended that children's care should be divided among separated caregivers in the same ratio that it was shared prior to the separation.

The contemporary Best Interests of the Child (BIC) ethic eschews all of these, in favor of a postseparation division of child care that is uniquely suited to the child's needs and the family's circumstances. Although the BIC ethic pervades today's legal system and has become the touchstone of child-centered professional organizations from the United Nations to the American Medical Association, no one has yet adequately defined it. As much as we may seek to serve the best interests of our children, we don't yet know what they are.

The Child's Needs Versus the Child's Wishes

What we do know is that our children's wants and needs are often quite distinct.

We also know that our kids often don't know this about themselves.

The psychological attributes that allow mature adults to know what they *need* and how this is different from what they *want* only develop slowly and well into adulthood. Building the ego strength (the emotional *oomph!*) necessary to seek to fulfill your needs even at the cost of your wants is a goal that some adults never attain.

You know, for example, that you need to eat your vegetables, exercise daily, complete your work on time, floss regularly, and get more sleep. This knowledge is a developmental success in and of itself. Whether or not you actually *do* these things, recognizing the *wants* that you forego along the way (eating ice cream while watching a ball game on the couch, avoiding work—or is that what you're doing right now?) is one test of genuine social and emotional maturity.

These and related skills blossom slowly, unevenly, and idiosyncratically in our children as a function of some combination of genetics, temperament, and experience. "Experience," in this case, refers largely to the model that you and your co-parent have provided for your child. It is thus sadly the truth that the kids whose future care is most likely to be at issue may be among those least well prepared to offer a mature opinion in the matter.

Of course, age makes a difference as well. Older children are reasonably expected to be more socially and emotionally (and physically) mature than younger children. But the relationship between chronology and social and emotional (as opposed to physical) maturity is weak. Laws that are age-based (driving at sixteen, voting at eighteen, drinking at twenty-one, and, in some states, being heard on the subject of your own postdivorce care at twelve or fourteen) are misleading at best, and outright dangerous at worst.

Many professionals have advised that children should never be put in a position to voice an opinion about their own postseparation care. This is contrary to many conflicted caregivers' beliefs that their custodial dispute could be settled "if you'd just listen to the kids!"

Why not allow children to decide with whom they live and when? Because we know that they can't reliably see the distinction between what they need and what they want. Here's why:

1. *Children think in me-here-now terms.* This self-centeredness is, as it should be, the natural complement of the healthy parent's selfless focus on my-kids-first-and-always. The capacity to look beyond yourself and take in another person's perspective, and then to respond empathically, develops slowly and well into early adulthood.

2. *Children tend to be impulsive.* Learning to think first, to weigh alternatives, to consider consequences, and to avoid unnecessary risks are signs of emerging maturity. These, together with the abilities to delay gratification, establish long-term priorities, and plan ahead, develop gradually when the world is predictable and consequences are contingent.

3. *"Dessert first!"* When faced with a choice between something that will make a child happy and something that will make a child healthy, most children (and many adults!) will choose the thing that makes them happy. This opens the door to the Disneyland Dad dilemma, discussed in Chapter 10.

4. *Children want to earn their parents' affection and approval.* This is true even during adolescence (when it can be hardest to

detect) and long into adulthood for most of us. Being caught in the middle means, in part, feeling that you cannot earn one parent's affection and approval without losing that of the other.

5. *Autonomy and identity are at risk.* We are all born unable to distinguish self from nonself. The newborn's experience of hunger and food, pain and comfort, self and other are undifferentiated. Growing up is thus a process of separating and defining boundaries. Having to choose between Mom and Dad either because they are tacitly demanding it or because the court is explicitly requesting it forces a premature separation that can have profound consequences for the child's emerging sense of self.

6. *Stress induces regression.* Even if an objective measure of social and emotional maturity were available, the most mature child cannot be expected to fulfill this potential under the intense emotional pressures inherent in the task of choosing between her parents.

How Can We Determine What Our Kids Need?

If the people who are supposed to know a child the best—her parents—disagree about her future care, and if the child cannot and should not make the choice herself, what's the alternative?

A flip of a coin?

Best two out of three rock-paper-scissors throws?

Or perhaps Solomon's method should become the law. The biblical king resolved two women's dispute over a child's care by drawing his sword and determining to give each an equal half. The woman who objected the loudest was acknowledged to be the child's genuine mother because who else would care so intensely for a child's pain?

Letting the Courts Decide

When co-parents separate and contest their child's subsequent parenting plans, then lawyers are hired, papers are filed, and hearings are scheduled. The cast of characters increases by multiples of two as each side lines up witnesses and hires experts. The costs increase exponentially to the point of compromising the adults' savings, equity, and retirement security, and the child's education, at the least. Ironically, more than one parent has depleted his material resources in the course of trying to win a child's care by virtue of the many resources he has to offer.

The frank reality is that most courts and the professionals who fill them are trained to approach postseparation care disputes from the outmoded perspective of "custody" and in the court's more typical guilty-versus-innocent mind-set. Rather than seeking to establish how best to meet a particular child's needs, a battle ensues over which parent will win and which will lose. The parents are no longer parents but "parties," each trained by the zealous advocate of their choice to put on their own Sunday best even while attempting to make the other look as despicable as possible. In this supercharged, kill-or-be-killed environment, molehills become mountains. A late pickup becomes an act of neglect, a firm consequence becomes an act of abuse, and an innocent bathroom mix-up (*"Dad, I'm changing!"*) becomes reason for an emergency ex parte removal order. Any word or action, present or past, can be taken out of context and put under a magnifying glass in the "best interests of the child."

Statistics suggest that the divorce process in the United States generally takes one full year to complete from initial filing through final hearing. This average is misleading, however, because it includes the vast, silent majority of healthy co-parents who settle their differences quickly and the frequent-triers, the revolving-door litigants, those intractably conflicted co-parents who replace undying love with unending litigation. The conventional wisdom relates that this most highly conflicted 10 percent among co-parents consumes 90 percent of the court's time. Some return to court dozens and even hundreds of times over a period that might go on forever, were it not for the eventual celebration of the child's eighteenth birthday.

No one knows what becomes of the children raised in such an environment.

In fairness, the family court judge faces a near-impossible task: sorting through hours upon hours of testimony and paperwork weighed by the pound in order to administer justice. Many do the job extraordinarily well, despite the gut-wrenching emotions, procedural constraints, and pitiful budgets that characterize most courts. The judge's position seated front and center, often at a raised desk, often in a black robe, gavel in hand, is more than just pomp or presumption. The total psychological effect is one of finality and decisiveness. The court's ruling is final. The matter is closed. Structure has been imposed, and structure, we all know, decreases anxiety.

Somewhere in between the quick-settling majority and the recidivist minority is a population of moderately conflicted co-parents. These former intimate partners may be unable to resolve their differences even with the able assistance of a therapist or a mediator, but risk becoming further polarized by an adversarial court system. For these co-parents, there may be two reasonable alternatives to better understanding and meeting their children's postseparation needs.

Experts, Experts, and More Experts

The unstated fact is that very few professionals affiliated with the court system are trained in the areas most relevant to postseparation child-care decisions: child development, family dynamics, mental health, parenting, and co-parenting. There are, of course, those few mental health professionals who are certified to serve as guardians ad litem. Others have undergraduate or even advanced degrees in mental health and go on to subsequently become attorneys and may even serve as judges. But, for the most part, the legal professionals to whom we entrust our kids' futures know little more about children than the lessons they learned raising their own.

This is a good argument for introducing expert witnesses into family law courtrooms. An expert witness is a professional who has the credentials and the experience necessary to educate the court on a matter relevant to the litigation. Experts are commonly introduced into civil suits, for example, as when a physician is hired to evaluate a complainant for the purpose of informing the court about the extent of injury endured due to an institution's neglect.

A child-centered professional with established credentials serving as an expert can help the court make sense of the mountain of testimony and evidence accumulated in the course of litigation. For example, if Mom argues that Sally should be using an inhaler for her asthma and Dad responds that Sally has no such illness and that no medication is necessary, it may only be after a pediatric pulmonologist (kids' lung doctor) is brought in as an expert that the court will be able to make sense out of their differences.

Unfortunately, when one parent introduces an expert in support of her position, the other parent may do the same, serving only to escalate the layers of confusion and the costs of the process. For this reason, experts who are invited to address matters relevant to a child's future care will often (and probably should) request that they be allowed to enter the fray in a neutral or child-centered but unallied and impartial role. This is perhaps best accomplished by having the court (in the person of the guardian ad litem) introduce the expert whose opinions can then be solicited via deposition and cross-examination by both sides.

In some cases, an expert can provide general information that serves to help the court to interpret the testimony and documentation already before it. Litigation that includes a disagreement about home schooling, for example, might well benefit from expert testimony on the academic achievement of home-schooled as opposed to public- or private-schooled children. Independent and neutral facts documenting that the graduates of one type of education routinely achieve better than the graduates of the others could very well sway the court's interpretation of the contending parents' respective plans, even though the expert may never have spoken with the parties or their children.

In other cases, experts are hired to assess and subsequently to educate the court about factors that are entirely specific to the matter at hand. Allegations suggesting that one or both caregivers abuse drugs or alcohol; act out violently; or have a relevant psychological, physical, or learning disability (among many others) are routinely better addressed by evaluating experts than by arguing attorneys.

Thus, the first alternative to engaging in an escalating court battle is to ask an expert to advise the court regarding the child's needs and the optimal postseparation parenting plan by conducting a child-centered family evaluation.

Neutral Experts

In the course of working with marriage therapist, Dr. Brilliant, Adam's and Eve's stories about their son's high activity level and distractibility prompted a referral to child psychologist, Sarah Smiley. Dr. Smiley evaluated the child and, despite the fact that he was only three years old at the time, diagnosed him as having attention-deficit/hyperactivity disorder (ADHD).

This matter became very controversial when the parents ended up in court arguing over their son's future care. Would the child's ADHD better suit him to living primarily with Mom or primarily with Dad? Would he be better off with frequent transitions back and forth between homes or with longer periods of stability in each? The lawyers argued for the interpretations that best suited their respective clients, but in truth, none were ADHD experts.

Adam's attorney called Dr. Smiley and offered to hire her as

Neutral Experts *(continued)*

an expert witness for the purpose of educating the court about ADHD and its possible bearing on the child's future care. Dr. Smiley agreed that she was qualified to address these questions and that the information could be quite valuable to the legal process, but asked if she could instead be hired by the court so as to remain neutral with regard to the adult's conflict. Failing that, she advised that even though Adam might foot the bill, her testimony would not necessarily support the father's wishes.

Adam's attorney motioned the court, a brief hearing was held, and everyone agreed that Dr. Smiley would be introduced as the guardian ad litem's witness, neutral to the adult conflict and her costs would be borne equally by the parties.

A Child-Centered Family Evaluation (CCFE)

One very specific type of expert assessment is known alternatively as a "custody evaluation," a "family systems assessment," or "a child-centered family evaluation" (CCFE). Regardless of the label, the process is intended as a comprehensive assessment of each of the participants, the quality of their interrelationships, and the relevant contextual factors that may bear on recommending to the court the optimal postseparation parenting plan.

A CCFE is a time-intensive, intrusive, and emotionally demanding snapshot of the family at its worst, torn apart and fighting to create new and healthier postseparation boundaries. It is a threatening, eye-opening, and expensive process, but, when done right, it is not only worth its cost in courtroom agony avoided but it is routinely less expensive than the attorney's fees and lost income that are typically associated with drawn-out litigation.

For all of its very real value, CCFE is not to be mistaken as a cure-all or as a scientifically reliable and valid instrument. Unlike the repeatable precision of an engineer's measurements or the demonstrable (if not uniform) benefit of a medication, the nature and process of CCFE can be highly controversial and, as such, can become subject to subsequent litigation itself.

The difference between a CCFE that helps and a CCFE that hurts rests in three factors: (1) the qualifications, experience, and presentation of the evaluator(s); (2) the terms of the evaluation established long before the process begins; and (3) the composition of the evaluation itself.

1. *The qualifications, experience, and presentation of the evaluator(s).* A CCFE requires the intense commitment of a mental health professional (or a team of mental health professionals) with special training in the overlap between psychological and legal systems, a field known as forensics. A forensic mental health professional has established expertise in child and family development, relevant legal standards and practices, and the use and interpretation of psychometric (that is, standardized psychological measurement) instruments.

   If you are considering participating in a child-centered family evaluation, it is critically important to choose the evaluator carefully. Among the many questions to consider are these:

a. What is his training? What continuing education courses has he attended or taught? Request a copy of his curriculum vitae (CV). How might these factors bear on his approach to the process?

b. Ask to receive copies of articles he's published and of talks that he's given. Check out his website. Try to determine what general conclusions and positions he's advocated in his publications.

c. How many such evaluations has he completed? With what age children?

d. What is his experience with the unique (medical, educational, psychological) needs relevant to your kids? What is his experience in relation to yourself and your co-parent?

e. With what assumptions and biases does he approach the process? Is he looking at the least detrimental alternative? Does he make a tender years presumption or take the approximation approach? How does he define the BIC criteria? Does he have biases or prejudices about the role of men versus women as caregivers? Does he have biases or prejudices about relevant religious, ethnic, sexual orientation, or gender identity issues?

f. Does he have children himself? Is he married or divorced?

g. Is he willing and able to research factors that arise relevant to the evaluation? Will he look into the qualifications, for example, of each of two schools being considered for your child? Would he consider the relevance or irrelevance of Mom's thyroid condition and Dad's hypoglycemia on parenting potential?

h. Will he consult with colleagues? Will he speak with your therapist and your co-parent's therapist? What is his position on speaking with the child's therapist and the way that such an intrusion might or might not corrupt the child's experience of that therapy as her only remaining port in the storm?

Whether you have the opportunity to address these many preliminary questions face to face, by phone, in writing, or by proxy through your attorney, do what you can to reach a conclusion, as well, about the evaluator's personality. Entering the legal arena is not for the faint of heart. Conducting a CCFE calls for technical proficiency as well as a commanding presence and an authoritative presentation. You want to be confident that the evaluator has the patience and empathy to see into your children's thoughts and feelings, as well as the strengths necessary to confront you and your parenting partner on those little white lies and those larger, bold-faced denials. You want to work with someone who will write a clear and definitive report ("Can I see a CCFE report that you've written?") and someone who can, as necessary, follow that up with an unambiguous and commanding presentation in court.

2. *The terms of the evaluation established long before the process begins.* Once an evaluator or team of evaluators is agreed upon, the co-parents will be required to sign and return an agreement or contract intended to clarify fully the scope and limitations of the process. Sitting down to the first interview—or worse, participating in an extensive process—without such prior written agreement invites tremendous misunderstanding, confusion, damage, and cost later.

The initial CCFE agreement should, at a minimum, detail the following to your satisfaction:

a. What is the overall purpose or intent of the CCFE? Will it yield only a description of each participant ("Billy is a very angry boy") and leave the court to interpret these? Will it interpret observations ("Billy's extreme anger is related to his experience of his parents' conflicts"), or will it take the additional step of drawing recommendations from these data ("Billy will benefit from intense psychotherapy and from a care schedule that minimizes his exposure to the co-parents' continuing conflicts")?

b. Will these summary observations, interpretations, and recommendations be presented in the form of a written report? When can that report be expected? To whom will it be delivered? Once received, what is the procedure for subsequent discussion, feedback, or correction of factual errors? Will the evaluator meet with the co-parents to discuss the report?

c. Will the CCFE report make general recommendations regarding the co-parents' respective parenting responsibilities ("Because the co-parents remain highly conflicted, very much to Billy's detriment, one parent should be invested with legal decision-making authority, thereby minimizing the opportunity for conflict") or very specific "ultimate issue" recommendations ("Therefore, Mr. Smith should be vested with legal decision-making authority").

d. What are the limits of confidentiality during the course of the evaluation? What is the procedure if the evaluator believes that someone is in danger or a threat?

e. What are the costs, and how will they be divided? Will an initial retainer be necessary? If additional funding is necessary, how and when will the evaluator say so? Might health insurance cover any or all of these costs? (Probably not.)

f. What is the projected time course of the evaluation? Will it be completed before the next hearing? How might it be expedited or delayed? Are there any contingencies associated with either (savings or penalties, for example)? Does the agreement or contract expire at some time, invalidating the data collected to that point, requiring additional funds or a new contract, or terminating the process altogether?

3. *The composition of the evaluation itself.* As important as the preceding matters may be, the most common questions raised in advance of a CCFE are concerned with the how and when of the process. Participants reasonably want assurance that their case will be heard and that the evaluation will encompass each of the many factors unique to the child and her family circumstance.

Many variables distinguish one family's evaluation from another, not the least of which are the number of children, the distance between the homes, the presence of parenting partners (Grandma's role in one home; a roommate's role in the other), the role of extended family members, and the relevance of new intimate others. With this variability in mind, the composition and sequence of each CCFE must be individually determined. Nevertheless, each will typically include the following at a minimum:

a. Individual interviews with each parent, including thorough history and background, understanding of present concerns and goals, view of the co-parent, and view of the child in detail.

b. Joint interviews with the co-parents together, including their respective parenting partners if possible. These opportunities can be emotionally supercharged, but as long as there are no safety concerns (history of domestic violence, for example) or legal restrictions (restraining orders), they can be an invaluable source of information relevant to understanding the quality of co-parenting.

c. Firsthand observation of the child. How this is conducted will depend largely on the child's age, maturity, and circumstance. Infants and toddlers will seldom be observed in one-on-one interaction with the evaluator. Younger children might best be met at school or in the home so as to maximize comfort. Some children might usefully be engaged in play. Others might be interviewed directly.

d. Observation of each postseparation family group. This could mean joining Mom and daughter for supper in the home or inviting Dad and daughter, Dad's roommate, and Dad's older son by his former marriage—all of whom hope to live together as a family unit—into the office to talk and play.

e. Collection of auxiliary sources of information, including review of therapy, medical, and school records; court documents; correspondence; and interviews in person, by phone, or via written materials with personal references, employers, therapists, and friends.

The Collaborative Law (CL) Movement

Recognizing the dilemma implicit in approaching parenting and child-care matters with the same brute judicial force that can be necessary in criminal matters, the collaborative law (CL) movement was born. Today, CL has been accepted in more than half of the United States and much of Western Europe.

CL is a process of negotiation and compromise intended to assist minimally and moderately conflicted co-parents in settling their differences outside of the courtroom. The process requires that each co-parent hire a specially trained collaborative law attorney. The two contesting co-parents, together with their respective CL attorneys, meet to negotiate mutually acceptable outcomes. Neutral advisors (child development expert and financial specialist, for example) are sometimes brought in by mutual consent to assist in settling particular concerns.

The CL process is a civil, child-centered, and respectful process governed by five basic rules:

1. Everyone will be treated with respect and behave in good faith.
2. There are no secrets or secret agendas. The parents will freely disclose all relevant information.
3. Neither parent will take advantage of mistakes made by the other.
4. Should the case go to court, the CL lawyers will not litigate the case. The CL advocates will not divulge matters discussed in the process, and the parents will each hire new attorneys.
5. Matters discussed in the CL meetings remain confidential.

Because the CL process is based on constructive exchange and mutual respect, it can be tremendously helpful and financially efficient. It can serve to minimize or avoid entirely the polarizing, black/white effects often associated with the conventional legal process.

But CL is not for everyone. When substance abuse issues, serious mental health concerns, and domestic violence or child abuse/neglect concerns arise, CL may no longer be viable. In fact, when one adult feels threatened by another or when there are questions about a child's safety in either parent's care, the legal and physical protections afforded by the legal system may be the only reasonable course.

Chapter 12

The Anatomy of a Parenting Plan

W hether by mutual agreement in an out-of-court settlement, with the assistance of a therapist or mediator or collaborative law process, on the basis of a GAL's recommendations, as the result of a CCFE, or handed down from the bench with the crash of a gavel, the goal is to create a parenting plan: a child-centered schedule of parenting rights and responsibilities and associated contingencies. A parenting plan is a structure intended to help to settle everyone's anxiety, to diminish the opportunity for conflict and to make the child's world (and possibly our own, as well) more predictable and secure.

The goal is to keep the kids out of the middle.

As the architects of your children's future, how do you start to create a parenting plan?

Start by determining whether your state or jurisdiction recommends or requires a specific postseparation or postdivorce parenting plan format. The easiest way to do this is to call any attorney's office advertising divorce or family law in the phone book or to call or Google the local or state seat of government (town hall, for example). The question that you want to ask one way or another is, "Does the town/county/city/state have a template for custody orders?"

This chapter provides child-centered guidelines that can be useful when creating or critiquing a parenting plan. These are the general rules of thumb that some child-centered professionals agree are relevant to meeting children's postseparation needs and to keeping them out of the middle.

When Co-Parents Cooperate and When Co-Parents Conflict

The quality of the relationship among co-parents is the single best predictor of a child's future mental health and among the most important determinants of the postseparation parenting plan.

All other things being equal, children who are raised by cooperative co-parents are physically and emotionally healthier, more successful in the workplace, go on to create healthier relationships, and become healthier parents themselves.

All other things being equal, cooperative co-parents can establish a more open-ended and flexible postseparation parenting plan, confident that they will be able to respond to the hundreds of dilemmas, opportunities, challenges, and crises that are bound to arise (sometimes all at once, sometimes spaced across a lifetime) in the course of raising a child.

The flip side of that coin is also true: caregivers who are mutually unable to communicate, cooperate, and put their children's needs first, before their own needs, must have a rock-solid, set-in-stone, extremely detailed, concrete, and inflexible parenting plan. Why? Because in the absence of child-centered collaboration none of those hundreds of normal and expectable fires will be put out. Instead, each one risks becoming another war in which the only victims will be the children.

Conflicted caregivers need more structure. Cooperative caregivers need less.

"I cooperate! She doesn't!"

Good. You're taking the high road as you should.

But when it comes to creating a parenting plan, the answer can never be one-sided. Either the co-parenting team as a whole is able to put the child's needs first, or it isn't. Period.

Take This Test: How Child-Centered Is Our Co-Parenting Team?

The best predictor of the future is the past.

The best way to know whether the co-parenting team will be flexible, responsive, child-centered, and consistent is whether it acted that way yesterday or last month or last year.

"But things have changed!" you object.

Of course they have. They always do.

Here's an unscientific survey that you and your co-parent can use to assess the quality of your co-parenting. Because "things have changed" and are probably still changing since the intimate adult relationship ended, you may want to use this survey a number of times to check on how those things are changing: Is the co-parenting team improving toward genuinely child-centered collaboration? Is it stagnant and stuck in a rut? Or is it perhaps losing ground, sliding down the slippery slope of escalating conflict, renewed litigation, and growing pressure on the kids?

To Complete This Survey

Co-parenting is defined by its four component skills: (A) child-centeredness, (B) communication, (C) consistency, and (D) mutual alignment. There are six statements under each skill category and twenty-four statements in all. You and your co-parent should each *separately* rate all twenty-four statements on a scale of 0 to 4 defining, whether in your view,

0 = This statement is never true about our co-parenting.

1 = This statement is rarely true about our co-parenting.

2 = This statement is sometimes true about our co-parenting.

3 = This statement is often true about our co-parenting.

4 = This statement is always true about our co-parenting.

(A) Child-centeredness

This co-parent and I . . .	Never				Always
Put our children's needs first	0	1	2	3	4
Treat the children as friends	0	1	2	3	4
Understand what our children want and need	0	1	2	3	4
Argue about which of us is right	0	1	2	3	4
Stay in touch with the children's teachers and doctors	0	1	2	3	4
Cannot talk about the children	0	1	2	3	4

(B) Communication

This co-parent and I . . .	Never				Always
Communicate with one another about the children	0	1	2	3	4
Make plans for the children without informing each other	0	1	2	3	4
Know how to reach one another at all times	0	1	2	3	4
Ask the children to communicate adult information to their other parent	0	1	2	3	4
Routinely share information about our children	0	1	2	3	4
Keep secrets about the children from one another	0	1	2	3	4

(C) Consistency

This co-parent and I ...	Never				Always
Present a united front to the children	0	1	2	3	4
Have separate rules and limits for the children	0	1	2	3	4
Support one another's parenting decisions	0	1	2	3	4
Approach parenting differently	0	1	2	3	4
Follow through with the other parent's decisions for the children	0	1	2	3	4
Ignore or disregard each other's parenting decisions	0	1	2	3	4

(D) Mutual Alignment

This co-parent and I ...	Never				Always
Speak positively about one another to the children	0	1	2	3	4
Ask the children to choose between us	0	1	2	3	4
Respect each other as parents	0	1	2	3	4
Ask the children to keep secrets from their other parent	0	1	2	3	4
Know that the children are well cared for with the other parent	0	1	2	3	4
Insult or curse one another around the children	0	1	2	3	4

To score this survey: The survey will yield four separate scores, one representing the co-parenting team's mutual ability in each of the four skill categories. It will also yield a total co-parenting quality index. Calculate the sum for each of the four skill categories in this way:

1. *Reverse the scores for the shaded items.* The shaded statements describe behaviors that are contrary to healthy co-parenting. This means that the scores for each shaded statement must be subtracted from 4. For example, if you responded to "This co-parent and I approach parenting differently" by marking 3, calculate the reverse by subtracting 3 from 4. The reverse score for this response is $4 - 3 = 1$.

2. *Sum the scores within each skill category.* Add up your three responses for the unshaded statements for each category plus the *reverse* scores for the three shaded statements within that category. This total will be between 0 and 24.

3. *Sum the two co-parents' scores for each skill category.* When Mom and Dad, for example, complete this survey, Mom's sum for Consistency is added to Dad's sum for Consistency. This total will be between 0 and 48.

To make sense out of these results: Lower numbers (approaching 0) in each of the four skill categories represent co-parenting weaknesses. Higher numbers (approaching 48) represent co-parenting strengths. As a general guideline, any skill receiving a combined total score between 33 and 48 is quite strong. A score in this range is a very reassuring message that the safety net beneath your child is secure and that your child has good reason to feel confident.

A combined skill score between 25 and 32 suggests some weaknesses. There are holes in the safety net that may be putting your kids in the middle, leaving them insecure and at risk for unnecessary upset. Start stitching these holes together by recognizing them. Talk them through with your co-parent if you're able. Reread the chapters in this book that address each of the skills:

- Child-centeredness is the subject of the entire book. It is addressed directly in Chapter 11, for example.
- Communication is the subject of Chapter 13.
- Consistency is discussed in the Introduction.
- Mutual alignment is the subject of Chapter 12.

A combined score for any one or more of the four skill categories that falls in the range between 0 and 24 is a serious red flag for the co-parenting team and for your child's well-being. If, in fact, the co-parenting team is doing this poorly, then immediate assistance may be necessary. Ideally, the co-parents will mutually participate in a facilitated co-parenting intervention or mediation or seek out a parenting coordinator for the purpose of settling some of these critical differences. In addition, either the child's existing psychotherapist should be alerted that the co-parenting team is struggling, as that may help direct the course of the ongoing therapy, or it's finally time to arrange for your kids to see a psychotherapist because they're at high risk. Even if it doesn't show, these kids are very likely caught in the middle.

The co-parenting quality index is the sum of both co-parents' responses across all four skill categories (remember to reverse the numbers for the shaded items!). This composite will range between 0 and 192. Although this overall index is too broad to suggest constructive next steps for co-parents who want to improve their skills in their children's best interests, it can be useful in the process of creating a parenting plan.

The higher the co-parenting quality index, the less detailed and more flexible the parenting plan can be. Co-parents with high total scores are able to respond constructively to meet their children's needs. By contrast, as the co-parenting index falls toward 0, the parenting plan must become more and more detailed, specific, and concrete with as little room left for interpretation—and therefore conflict—as possible.

What Should We Include in the Parenting Plan?

A successful parenting plan is child-centered, even when its details conflict with the needs of the adults. It is proactive and foresighted, anticipating the child's growth and change in the future. A successful parenting plan serves the child's needs and clarifies the parents' respective responsibilities for meeting those needs both in the present and in the future.

Sound familiar? It should. A successful parenting plan is a structure that serves to decrease the anxiety between co-parents and thereby diminishes the opportunity for conflict. It calls for consistency and boundaries. It sets limits and establishes routines.

A successful parenting plan weaves a safety net under the co-parents so that the co-parents, in turn, can weave a safety net beneath their kids. Such a plan should address each of these variables as clearly and thoroughly as possible:

1. *Decision-making authority* (sometimes known as "legal custody"). How will the important decisions (school choice or

elective surgery, as examples) in my child's life be decided? If it
is to be shared between co-parents, what happens when we disagree? Is there a tie-breaking mechanism or arbiter? If there are
pockets of high conflict (psychotherapy or medication, for
example), can decision-making authority for these issues be
assigned unilaterally while all other major life decisions are shared?

2. *Routine residential responsibility* (sometimes known as "physical custody"). Where will the children live and on what schedule
during the typical school year? The *where* of residential responsibility defines who serves as the parent-on-duty or POD, the
caregiver who will be responsible for day-to-day decisions (such
as bedtime) even when the child is away (at summer camp, for
example). The *when* of residential responsibility defines the days
and times of day during which each caregiver fulfills this role.

3. *Exceptions to the routine residential responsibility schedule.*
These anticipate the child's care needs during typical school
vacations (summer, fall, winter, and spring), the common
holidays (Labor Day, Halloween, Thanksgiving, Christmas/
Hanukkah/Kwanzaa, New Years Day, Memorial Day, Independence
Day), any holidays specific to one or both of the parents' beliefs
(Yom Kippur, Ramadan, Chinese New Year), long weekends, and
teacher conference days. Addressing each of these individually may
be necessary for some. For others, general rules of thumb may suffice. For example: "Monday and Friday holidays, teacher workshops,
snow days, and other occasions that delay or cancel school will auto-
matically be appended to the responsibilities of the POD for the
adjoining weekend."

Vacations may need to be defined in terms of (a) how many overnights in a row a child will be allowed to be away from the other parent as a function of age or maturity (as discussed later in this chapter), (b) limitations of where a vacationing parent and child might travel (distance from home? overseas?), and (c) how long in advance the dates of the proposed vacation need to be established. The latter can be especially tricky given the vagaries of travel planning (air and hotel booking, for example) as these might compete with the child's schedule (tennis lessons) and the other parent's plans.

Consider, as well, addressing residential responsibility "what if?" contingencies now, to avoid as much confusion later as possible. What if the POD has to be away for a day or an overnight or longer? Who will take care of the kids? This is sometimes called the "right of first refusal," a contingency that allows the other parent the first option to resume parenting responsibilities if the parent-on-duty is unavailable for more than a predefined period.

4. *The absent parent's communication with the child* (and vice versa). Some caregivers find a co-parent's call (e-mail, IM, text message, video conference, carrier pigeon, or smoke signal) to their child disruptive, while others have no objection to this practice. Some caregivers want an absent parent's calls to their child to be scheduled within a narrow window of opportunity, while others offer no opinion on the matter. Most important among these considerations, however, is what communication between a child and an absent parent means to the child.

A child who is reassured by being allowed access to an absent parent might benefit from open access or the greater security of knowing that Mommy will always answer her phone between such and such hours. By contrast, a child who uses this access to call to be rescued from a conflict with the POD ("Daddy, Mommy's being mean again!"), to avoid responsibilities (chores, homework), or to interrupt routines (bedtime) likely needs a different schedule of access or different limits.

5. *Transitions.* A successful parenting plan clarifies the details of the child's transitions between caregivers, often the point of greatest vulnerability as the conflicted parties come face-to-face. Should routine transitions occur face-to-face or through a scheduled intermediary person (the child's therapist) or agency (the school)? When an intermediary is used, what should be done with the child's belongings?

Do face-to-face transitions need to be scripted (see Chapter 9)? How will transportation be orchestrated? Is it reasonable to expect that only the co-parents will drive, or are their friends, partners, and surrogates (a babysitter, for example) acceptable? Is it okay to have other people present at the transitions (boyfriend, the child's half-sister, play date)? A very specific and restrictive transition expectation might be stated like this:

Residential responsibility will change at noon on Wednesdays. The parents will transition through school whenever possible. The sending parent will drop Billy at school on Wednesday morning and leave his bags with the school counselor. The receiving parent will collect Billy and his belongings at the end of the school day on Wednesday. In any instance in which transition through school is not possible, the sending parent will deliver Billy to the receiving parent's home at twelve noon. Transition will occur in the receiving parent's driveway. The co-parents will engage one another according to the transition script developed with their co-parenting facilitator.

6. *Co-parent communication.* How will the co-parents keep one another up to date about matters relevant to the child's life? This includes the constant and necessary flow of minutiae (school play practices, birthday party invitations) as well as important details (dentist's appointment, medication change) and urgent matters such as injury or illness.

Establishing a structured, routine communication may suffice for some of these matters ("The sending parent will complete an update chart in advance of the transition") specifying that the child must not be put in the middle ("and will deliver it directly into the hand of the receiving parent or his or her adult proxy"). Time-sensitive and urgent matters may need to be communicated in a different way ("In case of a sudden illness, injury, or an emergency that bears on the child's well-being or on the schedule of residential responsibilities, the POD will attempt to notify the other parent directly by phone, calling first to the work number, next to the home number, and finally to the cell number, leaving a succinct message at each point as possible.")

7. *Mutual alignment.* Co-parents who need a parenting plan may

need the obvious spelled out as clearly as possible: "Neither parent nor their respective friends, family, and associates will say or do anything which denigrates the other parent directly or indirectly, to or around the children. The parents acknowledge that any such selfish behavior constitutes abuse."

8. *The value of the sibling group.* When co-parents share responsibility for more than one child, the relationship between the siblings must be taken into account, taking special care that normal sibling rivalry not be mistaken for genuine conflict and, in separating the kids, deprive them of the critical emotional support each provides the other. Should the kids transition together? What are the conditions in which they might be separated?

9. *Children grow up.* A successful parenting plan must adapt to the child's gradually shifting needs and abilities. This may mean that the parameters set forth throughout the document are tied to the child's age ("The child may vacation with the POD for a number of consecutive nights not to exceed twice her age in years") or grade. In this case, the child's opinion or wishes are given different weight over time.

10. *The child's discretion.* One of the stickiest wickets that conflicted co-parents can face is how much discretion a child can be granted in determining with whom she lives. A successful parenting plan determines when, if, and how a child's preferences can be heard, stating, for example, that, "The child's preference for her own residential care as stated to the POD will be communicated between co-parents in a timely manner. It is only with the co-parents' mutual agreement that such a preference can be honored."

11. *Conflict resolution alternatives.* Finally, a successful parenting
plan anticipates that conflicts will arise. Loopholes in the best parenting plans are discovered and previously unimagined circumstances (diagnosis of a serious illness, a job offer overseas,
revelation of a new sexual orientation or identity) do occur. Just
as many corporations provide employees with a sequence of steps
to follow to voice a grievance, co-parents may need a prescribed
sequence of steps to follow to resolve a conflict, for example:

When a conflict arises, the co-parents will address it immediately, so as to minimize the likelihood that it will unnecessarily
develop into an emergency. In the first instance, the co-parents will
seek to resolve the issue in direct discussion away from the child.
Failing this, the matter will be taken to the co-parenting facilitator
or mutual therapist. Failing that, the parenting coordinator (PC)
will be empowered to investigate and arbitrate. Should the PC be
unable to reach a conclusion, unwilling to address the matter
because it falls beyond his expertise or contracted limits, or should
the PC's decision remain disputed, only then can the matter be
brought before a court. The parent pursuing this most extreme rem-
edy may be held responsible for the full costs of the process at the
court's discretion.

Filling Loopholes and Avoiding Ambiguity: Tricks and Tactics to Get Started

Keeping in mind that a successful parenting plan must be as unique
as the kids whom it serves, it is still possible to suggest a handful of
general guidelines with which to begin your thinking. None of these

are scientific truths or immutable facts. None are presented here as statistically reliable or valid parenting practices; in fact, there is little or no data with which to even approach that discussion. The positions that follow are simply a few among the many tricks and tactics that have proven useful for some co-parents as they begin the discussion about how to craft their parenting plan:

1. *Even/odd rules.* When a parenting plan calls for choices to be made (scheduling summer vacation with the kids, for example), conflicted co-parents will argue about whose choice should be given priority. This problem can be avoided when the parenting plan explicitly grants one parent priority in even-numbered years and the other parent priority in odd-numbered years.

2. *A default driver?* Conflicts often arise around transportation at the point of transition. Parenting plans that use the terms "sending parent" and "receiving parent" avoid some of these issues by stipulating either a default ("In case of dispute, the sending parent will transport the child") or an absolute ("The sending parent will always transport the child").

3. *Transition through school* (or camp, church, or the child's therapy hour) can be useful when the co-parents' face-to-face encounters may be explosive, but are prone to create ambiguities about who has responsibility for the child during the intervening school day. A good rule of thumb to spell out in your parenting plan is as follows: "The sending parent relinquishes residential responsibility and the receiving parent assumes it upon drop-off at the start of the school day." Alternatively: "Even when the child transitions through an intermediary agency

(school, for example), the parents' respective responsibilities transition at twelve o'clock noon."

4. *Playground politics.* The idea that the child should never be made a courier between his parents is critically important and just one way to keep him out of the middle. Co-parents who try to squeeze through a loophole on this one often end up in trouble. Putting the support check, the transition update, the latest "How dare you!" letter or court document in the five-year-old's backpack is an invitation for the entire class to read it on the playground or the bus ride.

5. *U-Store-It.* The dilemma of transporting a child's possessions between homes when transition occurs through an intermediary arises again and again ("But what do I do with his football gear?"). When drop-off at the receiving parent's home isn't acceptable, it is sometimes worthwhile to rent a self-storage space at a mutually convenient location. In this way, the sending parent and the child can stop by the storage space on the way to school, drop off belongings so they're not carried to school (avoiding the child's humiliation concerns, as well) and go on their way. The receiving parent can collect the belongings any time thereafter in advance of pickup or with the child later in the day. Put a separate mailbox or lockbox in the storage space and adult papers can go back and forth without falling into the child's hands.

6. *Suppertime calls.* It may seem convenient and desirable to schedule calls between the child and the absent parent at the child's bedtime, but beware: a child struggling with any degree of

separation anxiety or worry for the absent parent's well-being
risks being stirred up by this call when his emotional resources
are weakest, a situation that is not conducive to sleep.
Scheduling the contact just before leaving for school in the
morning can create a similar problem. When defining a contact
window is useful, the best time may be immediately after supper
in the POD's home.

7. *Signaling priority.* Co-parents who use e-mail to communicate
sometimes complain about a flood of messages, some of which
are trivial (if well-intentioned) and others of which are critically
important. A successful parenting plan can restrict each parent
to one message each day except in emergencies. Alternately, co-
parents can agree to flag their messages by writing in the subject
line "green," "yellow," or "red." A green message is routine ("She
ate all her vegetables"). A yellow message is important ("She
choked on a carrot, but she's okay. No medical treatment necessary."), and a red message is urgent ("She choked on a carrot. I
dialed 911, and an ambulance came. She's okay, but very scary.")
and should probably be followed up by a direct call.

8. *Introducing new partners.* When an intimate adult relationship
is ended, strong feelings often persist. These feelings can complicate the co-parenting relationship in a million small ways. This
can become particularly complicated when adults develop new
intimate relationships. Questions reasonably arise about how
and when to introduce the child to the new partner. One
approach is to establish in the parenting plan that: "Neither
parent will introduce the child to a new intimate partner before

that person is ready to become a part of the co-parenting team."

9. *Different sibling needs.* The sibling groups' value may suggest that the sibs remain together, but what about the differences in their needs and abilities due to their varied ages? This question expectably becomes more pronounced as the age range among brothers and sisters increases. As a general rule of thumb, decisions for the group as a whole should be made on the basis of the youngest (least emotionally mature) child's needs.

10. *How many transitions?* A parenting plan must be considered both in terms of how much time a child spends in each parent's care *and* in terms of the number of transitions the child must make between the two homes. As the number of transitions in a given period (two weeks, for example) increases, so, too, do a number of important considerations: (a) more time in transit means less time playing and exploring and making friends, not to mention sleeping and doing homework; (b) more opportunities for exposure to conflict when the co-parents transition face-to-face; (c) more total time invested in adjusting, including packing and unpacking; (d) more opportunities for co-parent communication to fail and, therefore, a greater likelihood of the kids becoming caught in the middle.

11. *Avoid ambiguity.* The more precise the language in the parenting plan, the less room for ambiguity and confusion. One common ambiguity arises around whether Mom's responsibility for Sally's care ends at 7:00 p.m. Sunday *and then* she is to drive her to Dad's home or whether, instead, Sally is expected to be delivered to Dad's home at 7:00. Because responsibility for a

child's care routinely involves chauffeuring hither and yon, this wording should dictate that Sally will return to Dad's care at the appointed hour.

12. *Count overnights, not days.* Children conceptualize periods of time in each home most easily when they are described in terms of numbers of nights or "sleeps." The language spelling out a parenting plan should therefore use the same terms. Plans that describe a parent as responsible for child care "for three consecutive days" are vulnerable to the same confusion that vacation advertisements capitalize upon ("Get away for a five-day/four-night adventure!"). Say "three consecutive overnights" instead.

Common Parenting Plans

A child-centered postseparation parenting plan is ultimately a balancing act. It is an imperfect, practical compromise seeking to juggle at least four competing factors:

- **Continuity care versus separation from the absent caregiver:** All other things being equal, a child who experiences separation anxiety while apart from her caregivers is better served by a parenting plan that allows for briefer stays with each. Conversely, a child who has the emotional maturity to tolerate longer separations may be better served by a plan that allows for longer stays with each.

- **Continuity of care versus the upset associated with transition:** All other things being equal, if a child is at risk for being exposed to renewed parental conflict when she transitions between homes, then her needs will be better served by a parenting plan that minimizes the frequency of transitions. Conversely, if transitions are conducted smoothly and with a minimum of stress, the parenting plan can allow for more frequent transitions.

- **Frequency of transition versus the consistency between the two homes:** All other things being equal, a child will be better served by a parenting plan that requires fewer transitions between homes that are quite different (different expectations, consequences, limits, and boundaries, for example). Conversely, a child will manage more frequent transitions between homes that are quite similar more easily.

- **Frequency of transition versus the quality of co-parent communication and cooperation:** All other things being equal, when co-parents communicate and cooperate successfully, the parenting plan can be more flexible and spontaneous, allowing for more frequent transitions. Conversely, when co-parents fail to communicate and cooperate, the parenting plan should be more rigid and less subject to negotiation, calling for fewer transitions.

Upon reviewing these four criteria, two things should be immediately obvious: first, these criteria may seem contradictory or even mutually exclusive. It's not uncommon, for example, for a child who suffers separation anxiety when apart from each caregiver and who therefore needs more frequent transitions between homes to experience intense distress when her parents' argue, therefore calling for less frequent transitions. Unfortunately, there are no simple solutions to these common dilemmas, leaving co-parents and their professional helpers struggling to strike the balance that best suits the child's needs.

Second, all other things are seldom equal. Real-life differences in the quality of the child's relationship with each parent, the parent's respective schedules and availability, the needs of the child's siblings and the benefit the child accrues from remaining with that sibling group, the physical distance and associated travel time between the two homes, benefits associated with enrollment in one school district as opposed to another, access to the child's extracurricular activities and peer group . . . all of these and many more factors must be weighed into the formula.

Given this complexity, it is therefore ironic that our best efforts to define a postseparation parenting plan specific to each child's needs generally yield a small handful of common schedules. The most common among these are described below, noting some of the strengths and weaknesses often associated with each. Each is also illustrated by a sample calendar. For ease of reference, the illustrations all use the same transition standards: School-day transitions are scheduled to occur directly after school (noted here as 3:00 P.M. and abbreviated as 3p). Non–school day transitions are set at 7:00 P.M. (abbreviated here as 7p), a time that often allows a school-aged child to share supper with the sending parent and to arrive home without interfering with bedtime.

The Single Base

Perhaps as a result of the approximation rule, perhaps as a result of the realities of the workplace, this postseparation parenting plan was once quite common. This plan suggests that children should reside primarily with Parent A (most usually Mom) and see the other parent on infrequent "visits." Specifically, Parent B assumes parenting responsibilities for the children alternate weekends, Friday after school through Sunday supper, and every Wednesday evening for a few hours.

	Sunday	Monday	Tuesday	Wednesday	Thursday	Friday	Saturday
Week #1	A	A	A	A B 3p–7p A	A	A B 3p	B
Week #2	B A 7p	A	A	A B 3p–7p A	A	A	A
Residential responsibility is assigned to Parent A or Parent B by letter. Parent B's time is shaded. Times indicate points of transition. Contiguous shaded or unshaded blocks indicate an overnight care period.							

The Single Base offers the advantage that children wake up in the same home (A) every morning for school. This can be particularly important for kids who struggle with organization difficulties and related learning differences and when co-parents live very far apart. This may also be a strong consideration when the caregiver with primary residential responsibility is the better organized and more academically focused of the two. In addition, the stability and consistency inherent in this plan are often desirable when the co-parents have very different parenting philosophies or communicate poorly by minimizing the communication necessary between caregivers.

The Single Base plan has the additional benefit of being very simple and easy to understand. Weekday events routinely fall under one parent's purview, eliminating the need to count weeks out on a calendar to answer the question, "Mom, can I study at Billy's next Thursday?" even though it is necessary to count out weekends ("Let's see: Dad's; Mom's; Dad's; Mom's . . ."). It does, however, pose a number of potential problems related to the infrequency and brief duration of the child's contact with Parent B. A missed Wednesday during Week #2 of this plan due to inclement weather, illness, or a schedule conflict can create a ten-day separation. Worse still, the infrequency of contact can set up Parent B to become a Disneyland Dad (see Chapter 10).

Parent B's complaints that this plan "is not fair" and accompanying calculations demonstrating that the child is only in his care for 18 percent of the time every two weeks ("and he's asleep much of that!") don't hold water. Parenting plans must never be created with the parent's needs in mind. The question must always be whether the plan meets the child's needs.

"But," you're thinking, "don't the kids *need* to see their parents?" Of course they do. How much of their time is spent with each parent matters far less, however, than the quality of the time spent together and how the child copes with the periods of absence in between.

Alternating Weeks

In an Alternating Weeks schedule, children spend the entirety of a week in one parent's care and then switch to spend the entirety of the following week in the other parent's care. In some implementations (as illustrated here) the children are given a midweek check-in with the other parent. This may be necessary for younger children who find seven consecutive overnights away from one caregiver emotionally taxing. It might be contraindicated when such a brief transition risks exposure to increased co-parental tension.

	Sunday	Monday	Tuesday	Wednesday	Thursday	Friday	Saturday
Week #1	A	A	A	A B 3p–7p A	A	A B 3p	B
Week #2	B	B	B	B A 3p–7p B	B	B A 3p	A
Residential responsibility is assigned to Parent A or Parent B by letter. Parent B's time is shaded. Times indicate points of transition. Contiguous shaded or unshaded blocks indicate an overnight care period.							

An Alternating Weeks schedule (particularly when the midweek check-in is eliminated) can strike a balance between maximizing the child's time with each parent and minimizing the number of transitions that the child must endure. This is particularly important when each transition is another opportunity to witness the caregivers' hostility.

This schedule can be desirable, as well, when co-parental consistency is poor. A child who migrates between two very different homes can be expected to endure a kind of culture shock immediately following each transition. When the child only has the opportunity to stay in each home briefly, the necessary adjustment period can consume the child's entire stay, leaving everyone involved frustrated and unhappy. A full week in each home may be long enough to manage the adjustment while still enjoying the remaining time in that home before the process repeats.

Beware that an Alternating Weeks plan can create important discontinuities for a child whose parents communicate poorly. School projects begun in one home are never completed. Medications begun in one home aren't followed up in the other. Habits, chores, and routines established in one home are quickly forgotten in the other, sometimes making something as mundane as learning to play the piano or as important as completing a course of antibiotics a challenge worthy of Sisyphus.

Split Weeks

A Split Weeks schedule establishes a similar ratio of child-care responsibilities with more frequent transitions. In this illustration, parents alternate responsibility for weekends and divide responsibility for the remainder of the school week into two parts, the division balanced over a two-week period. This Split Week schedule is sometimes referred to as a 4-3/3-4 schedule.

	Sunday	Monday	Tuesday	Wednesday	Thursday	Friday	Saturday
Week #1	A					A	
		B	B	A	A		B
	B 7p		A 3p			B 3p	
Week #2	B				A	B	
		A	A			B	A
	A 7p				B 3p	A 3p	

Residential responsibility is assigned to Parent A or Parent B by letter.
Parent B's time is shaded. Times indicate points of transition.
Contiguous shaded or unshaded blocks indicate an overnight care period.

A Split Weeks schedule may serve the needs of a younger or less emotionally mature child who needs frequent contact with each of two separated caregivers. In the 4-3/3-4 illustration provided here, the child is away from each caregiver no more than three consecutive nights.

This plan sometimes suits parents with professions that demand brief, intensive work schedules (airline pilots, nurses, and firefighters, as examples). All other things being equal, fitting a child's schedule to the parent's availability may be a reasonable way to meet the child's need for time with that parent.

The arguments against a Split Weeks schedule are many: this schedule requires multiple transitions in a relatively brief period of time. As such, it not only increases the child's potential exposure to the co-parental conflict, it can leave a child in a near-constant state of adjustment—never able to settle in—especially when consistency is poor. In addition, many children find a Split Week schedule difficult to grasp, making even short-term planning ("Billy, can you come over after school tomorrow?") challenging.

Alternate Days

It may be surprising how often this schedule is proposed and implemented. An Alternate Days plan is precisely what the term suggests, a constant back-and-forth co-parenting juggling act. A genuine Alternating Days plan requires a two week rotation as follows.

	Sunday	Monday	Tuesday	Wednesday	Thursday	Friday	Saturday
Week #1	A	B	A	B	A	B	A
	B 7p	A 3p	B 3p	A 3p	B 3p	A 3p	B 7p
Week #2	B	A	B	A	B	A	B
	A 7p	B 3p	A 3p	B 3p	A 3p	B 3p	A 7p
Residential responsibility is assigned to Parent A or Parent B by letter. Parent B's time is shaded. Times indicate points of transition. Contiguous shaded or unshaded blocks indicate an overnight care period.							

In a partial Alternating Days plan, one parent accepts responsibility for two consecutive nights, and the remaining five nights alternate between homes. In the following illustration, weekends (Friday and Saturday nights) are routinely Parent A's responsibility.

Sunday	Monday	Tuesday	Wednesday	Thursday	Friday	Saturday
A	B	A	B	A	B	A
B 7p	A 3p	B 3p	A 3p	B 3p	A 3p	
Residential responsibility is assigned to Parent A or Parent B by letter. Parent B's time is shaded. Times indicate points of transition. Contiguous shaded or unshaded blocks indicate an overnight care period.						

These Alternating Days parenting plans maximize transitions at the cost of stability in either home. The former plan (on the two-week schedule) creates a minimum degree of stability and possibly the greatest amount of confusion short of a completely spontaneous, ad hoc ("Do you want her tonight?") arrangement. The child living either of these two Alternating Days plans is at high risk for becoming a chameleon (see Chapter 14).

When co-parental conflict is minimal, and communication and consistency are both excellent, an Alternating Days plan can assure that very young and very emotionally immature children have the opportunity to reconnect with each of two parents often, which is a benefit.

Nesting

Parents wishing to give their children a maximum degree of stability—the benefits of a single neighborhood, a single school bus, and a single school district—sometimes discuss nesting as an alternative parenting plan. Nesting describes any schedule of shifting parenting responsibility in which the adults move in and out of the home, rather than requiring the children to switch between adult homes.

In addition to maximizing the child's stability, nesting is often seen as a cost savings. Because the child stays put, there is no need to duplicate physical resources (high chair, toys, computers). Each parent's nonparenting ("off-duty") home can be simple and small, with no need to pay for space for the kids. In one illustration of extreme postseparation cooperation, the co-parents share a single, simple "off-duty" apartment the same way that some flight attendants share the costs of maintaining a simple layover apartment in a hub city.

Unfortunately, this plan sounds better than it usually works out in real life. Adults who have ended an intimate relationship routinely discover that they need a place of their own, untouched by the other. Fears and accusations of snooping, jealousy, and resentment associated with new partners, and conflict growing out of simple matters like replacing the broken teapot or replenishing the breakfast cereal, quickly outweigh the benefits that the child presumably enjoys associated with physical stability.

Alternating Month, Semester, or Year Schedules

Parenting plans that grant each parent exclusive or near-exclusive parenting responsibility for extended periods are usually discussed (but seldom implemented) when parents live very far apart. The reality is that children who are old enough and mature enough to tolerate separations of this duration typically can't or won't tolerate extended separations from their school and peer group in any one location. To the extent that these plans also mean that a child is enrolled in two distinct schools or school systems, inconsistencies of curricula and instruction risk compromising (at least) achievement and grades.

Vacations Only

In those situations in which co-parents live very far apart, the time and cost of travel may make anything but a Vacations Only schedule prohibitive. As the label suggests, this parenting plan places the vast majority of day-to-day parenting responsibility in one caregiver's hands and allows that the child will spend extended vacation periods relatively infrequently with the other parent. In some instances, the absent parent travels to the child's hometown, takes a residential hotel room or suite, and fulfills parenting responsibilities from that temporary location. By entering the child's world, the visiting parent maximizes the child's physical stability and social connectedness at the cost of comfort and access to resources and opportunities in that parent's hometown. This plan can be particularly challenging when the absent parent is forced to leave a new family far away for the duration of the trip.

In other Vacations Only plans, the child travels some or all of the time to the absent parent's home and spends vacation time there.

A Vacations Only plan may be the only practical alternative when parents live far apart. It offers the benefit of maximizing a child's consistency and predictability in a single home at the cost of frequency of contact with the other caregiver. Travel expenses associated with this plan can be significant, but should not be a child's concern. Travel time, however, is a real cost that may be a concern to whomever is traveling, the parent or the child.

When the child travels, details—including the debate about the age at which a child can or should fly alone—commonly arise (although there is a growing population of children who spend nearly as much time in airports and on airplanes as they spend in school). Finally, the temptation for a parent to become a Disneyland Dad increases as the period of time between visits increases, risking undermining the hard-won structures in place in the child's primary residence.

Chapter 13

Keeping In Touch

Both the good news and the bad news is that contemporary electronic communications allow us to remain constantly in touch, no matter the distance, no matter the location, and no matter the message. The good news is that it is now neither expensive nor technologically difficult to share observations and ideas, to talk through a crisis, and to compromise and negotiate anywhere at any time. As a result, co-parents living on opposite sides of the planet can weave a safety net around their children, speaking in "we" statements about real-time, real-life events.

The bad news, of course, is that distance need no longer make the heart grow fonder because distance is no longer synonymous with separateness. Conflicted co-parents who cannot disengage—who insist on intruding into one another's lives, on flooding one another with insults, nosy questions, or inflammatory allegations—can do so easily and, in fact, do so quite commonly.

When an intimate adult relationship ends, the partners can choose to never speak together again. Mailing addresses, e-mail addresses, IM screen names, post office boxes, and phone numbers all can be changed with no harm done to anyone . . . unless they share children. As co-parents, these same partners hopefully have an interest and certainly have a responsibility to communicate. In fact, the success or failure of the co-parents' communications—keeping their communications child-centered and constructive, keeping the emotions generated by the failed adult relationship from leaking into that communication, and putting the available technologies to use in the best interests of their children—can be the difference between a child who is healthy and a child who is caught in the middle.

Kids As Couriers

It seems a simple solution. Two adults can't talk peaceably, so instead they let their kids bridge the communication gap across the dinner table, from behind one slammed door to the next, from one home to another. The kids become couriers:

"Ask your mom if . . ."

"Tell your dad that . . ."

But kids don't need to know all that grown-up stuff, right?

Okay, then stuff an envelope in her backpack or pin a note to his shirt. Don't kindergarten teachers do that all the time? Why shouldn't co-parents do the same to communicate with one another?

Because it puts the kids in the middle.

Making the kids into couriers gives them a burden that they aren't emotionally able to bear. It complicates the necessary tasks of child-hood—growing, exploring, playing, making friends, and learning—with an adult responsibility for no better reason than the parents' immaturity, selfishness, and convenience.

Asking your kids to communicate for you is like showing someone who is afraid of flying just how fragile and tentative the airplane wings really are. At first there's pride at being taken into an important person's confidence—that self-important feeling of being trusted by someone in authority. Then anxiety spikes. Confidence crumbles. That fragile sense of security is shattered as the reality hits.

The first time that you ask your child to play go-between, you'll see the same progression of emotions unfold. There's the initial pride of being promoted from foot soldier to lieutenant. Then the anxiety kicks in as worries, tummy aches, fears, or regressed acting-out emerge as she realizes what she actually has to do.

"Mom wanted me to give this to you . . ."

"Dad told me to tell you that . . ."

And then there are the questions of the efficiency and the accuracy of a message delivered by a child. The number of teacher conference notes, report cards, doctor and dentist appointment reminders, medication prescriptions, and assorted other detritus mulched into illegibility and forgotten in the bottom of kids' book bags and backpacks is beyond comprehension. A spoken message is likely to be treated even worse. When the message is remembered at all, it is subject to the same distortion and manipulation (See the next section on "splitting.") that anyone who has ever played the game called telephone knows so well. Something as simple as, "Tell your mom that 8:00 is fine," if not completely forgotten, is easily delivered as "Dad said I ate just fine," or "Dad wants you to know the eight are all mine," or even more likely, "Dad said to tell you something about a number . . ."

Hopefully you're wise enough not to blame the messenger ("How dare you talk to me that way, young lady!"). It's not your child's fault. True, she might be more responsible, but being responsible and following through are skills that she's still developing (even as a teenager!). Why would you trust something important to her limited and unreliable abilities when there is another way?

In fact, you don't need to blame the messenger. Tragically, this messenger will probably blame herself.

Your kids will blame themselves for your emotional pain. In that best-case scenario, however unlikely, when she actually remembers and delivers a not-so-mangled envelope from her other parent into your hands, she will blame herself for the emotions that cross your face as you read. Your anger, fear, or sadness may be a very reasonable reaction to the words that your co-parent wrote out, but she'll blame herself for causing them. Why not? If she hadn't delivered that envelope, you'd still be happy!

Compound this by responding in kind ("Then you tell your dad that . . . !" or "Okay . . . then you take this note back to that man!") and the cycle churns deeper and deeper into oblivion, round and round, as your child's mental health and well-being erode away.

The healthy, mature, and child-centered alternative is direct, adult-to-adult communication.

How? Read on.

On Splitting

Given the opportunity, your kids will split.

Mental health professionals use "split" to describe a third party's efforts to drive a wedge between two others—to "split" an existing alliance. In the context of co-parenting, splitting is one form of limit testing that occurs when a child's words or actions threaten to break down the alliance between caregivers in the interest of allying with one against the other. Splitting is a natural and normal event that healthy co-parents manage successfully most of the time simply by communicating.

Communication is the key.

When Billy complains, "You're mean. Mom let's me!" he's splitting. He's pitting you against your parenting partner. He's trying to guilt you into changing the limit that you've set ("No cookies for breakfast") or the expectation that you've stated ("bedtime at nine sharp") or the consequence that you've imposed ("Sorry, no computer privileges tonight"). He's asking, "Can I manipulate you?"

Here and now, it hardly matters whether Billy's mom actually does allow him to do whatever it is that he claims. What matters is how you respond while Mom's absent. Maybe she's gone fishing and will be back in an hour. Maybe she moved out three years ago and Billy sees her every other weekend.

"You're mean. Mom let's me!"

With hardly a thought, a healthy parent remains calm. He acknowledges the expressed emotion ("You're pretty mad") but stands firm ("That's how it's going to be"), providing incentive ("and if you can get it done before lunch, then we can ride bikes") and reassuring with an implicit "we" statement ("I'll check with Mom about next time"). The healthy parent's message reinforces the child's emotional security without fear of the child's anger ("I hate you!") and remains confident in his parenting partner's support.

"You're mean. Mom let's me!"

A conflicted co-parent hears and reacts to the same complaint very differently. Lacking a co-parent's support and respect—anxious, angry, guilty, and exhausted by the failed adult relationship—it's easy to lose perspective. It's easy to mistake the child's otherwise benign limit testing as a malignant threat that pushes all of your buttons and confirms all of your worst fears. A conflicted co-parent responds out of his own insecurities and, in so doing, fuels the child's insecurities. Another seam is torn down the middle of the child's safety net.

We all find it easier to believe a message that confirms an existing belief rather than a message that contradicts an existing belief. This is called confirmational bias. If you believe in UFOs, you're more likely to see one. If you believe today's your lucky day, it just might be.

If you believe that your parenting partner is too lenient or a pushover, you'll hear, "You're mean. Mom let's me!" as proof that she is. You'll think to yourself, *Of course she lets you! She'll let you do anything!* and your spoken reply will be angry, not reassuring: "I don't care what she says . . ."

You don't care what Mom says? Your anger at Mom doesn't belong here. By letting your anger at your former intimate partner contaminate your parenting, you're putting your kids in the middle. The co-parenting team has been split. Next thing you know, Billy will be telling Mom that he doesn't need to do what she says, "Because Daddy says that what you say doesn't matter!"

Then Mom's beliefs kick in. She hears Billy's statement not as a child's insolence or button pushing or splitting, but as a genuine echo of his father's assumed words. Her anger contaminates her response ("Well, you tell your father . . . !") and round and round they go, playing monkey in the middle with their beloved child, spiraling downward into oblivion.

Splitting in the Me-Here-Now

When co-parents don't communicate, splitting can become a very significant problem. If Sally tells Dad that she did her French project at Mom's and tells Mom that she did her French project at Dad's, Sally feels like she comes out ahead because she can be online at both houses without bothering with homework. She doesn't care that, in fact, she never did the French project and might fail the class. Why? Because Sally thinks in the me-here-now.

In the me-here-now, Sally's girlfriends are instant messaging each other in English (well, actually in a new alphanumeric dialect of English that most adults can't understand). They're definitely *not* speaking French, so why bother? Sally might have thought ahead far enough to know that when Madame sends home a note about the missed project, she can bury it in her book bag. And later when the report card is sent home? If Sally thinks that far, she probably realizes that she can tell Dad that she gave it to Mom and tell Mom that she gave it to Dad, and the subject will never come up again.

We must understand that *not* everything our kids say is true, no matter how much their words might confirm our implicit beliefs. Healthy co-parents put the child's needs first and bring the rest of the message back to one another directly and far away from the child.

"Billy told me that you . . ."

"Did you let Billy . . . ?"

"Here's what I heard. Can you help me understand . . .?"

When co-parents have enough trust and respect to communicate directly and constructively, there's a possibility that the problem can be worked out without escalating unnecessarily. Perhaps Billy is correct that Mom lets him even though Dad doesn't. Healthy co-parents identify their differences ("I think that he's old enough, and I did when I was his age. . . .") and try to reach an agreement for next time in the interest of consistency ("How about if we agree that he can on Saturdays?"). At the least, once differences are acknowledged, Billy's next complaint that "Mom let's me!" can be met with a well-informed and reassuring "we" statement: "I know. We've talked about it. That's what you do with her. This is what you do with me."

Unfortunately, rather than communicate, some co-parents try to compensate. Each hears the child's complaint as confirmation of their fears and beliefs about the other and leans in the other direction. The result is two homes that gradually become more and more polarized in a "Row, Row, Row Your Boat" situation.

Others take the bait entirely, so eager to confirm that the former intimate partner is evil that roles change. An alliance is created with the child at the cost of the alliance that should persist with the co-parent. In some instances, the child is inappropriately promoted to peer status by a parent eager for an ally in the war against the former partner. In other instances, the child is inappropriately made a parenting partner, responsible for younger siblings. In still other instances, the child is demoted to the status of a baby, fulfilling the needy parent's wish to nurture and be needed. These, respectively, are the dynamics of adultification, parentification, and infantilization.

Finding a Happy Medium

So how are we supposed to communicate? By not making the kids into couriers, that much is clear. The rest is a matter of media:

1. *The obvious first choice for constructive, child-centered co-parent communication is direct, face-to-face talking.* Co-parents who can sit down together over coffee, go for a walk together, or meet at the local bookstore on a regular basis are light years ahead of most. Face-to-face exchange allows so much more than just words to be communicated. Gestures, facial expressions, posture, and vocal tone together make every sentence richer and more meaningful. Unfortunately, this extra meaning can inflame the embers of adult conflict rather than work to a child's best interests, making face-to-face exchange less than constructive.

   Face-to-face meetings in public places can offer the additional advantage of helping participants remain civil. The fact that there are strangers nearby can create a kind of Big Brother effect (discussed later) that helps some adults keep their tempers in check.

   Be aware that direct co-parent communication (especially face-to-face meeting) can inadvertently fuel the kids' fantasies of reunion. If you're meeting every Tuesday at noon at the bookstore to talk, it may be best to tell the kids what you're doing. Otherwise they'll hear about these rendezvous and whisper secrets and hopes and pretty soon have you and their other parent back together.

2. *The second most efficient means of communication between co-parents occurs voice-to-voice by telephone or voice over Internet protocol* (VOIP). Voice-to-voice exchange carries all of the auditory nuances that might be helpful (or inflammatory) without demanding the travel or risking the proximity associated with face-to-face exchange. Setting aside the vagaries and frustrations of digital and cell technologies ("Can you hear me now?"), being available by cell at all times is at least a good emergency fallback upon which any co-parent can rely.

    Voice-to-voice calls may have the additional advantage of creating a record that a call was attempted or occurred when disputes over such things erupt. Face-to-face meetings, by contrast, rely on the variable memory of passersby, clerks, and wait staff if and when validation becomes necessary later.

3. *Somewhere among these top communication options is the relatively new and developing technology of video conferencing.* Although some large corporations use video conferencing routinely to tie colleagues together around the globe, at this writing only a small percentage of absent parents have begun using it to stay in touch with their kids. As webcams and technology (iChat, for example) become more common and accessible, co-parents can conceivably have all the benefits of face-to-face exchange without the risk that some associate with proximity and presum-

ably with much less risk of fueling children's fantasies of reunion.

4. *Real-time written electronic communications via e-mail, IM, or text messaging* can be a very efficient medium for co-parental communications, particularly when the nonverbal cues associated with face-to-face and voice-to-voice communications hurt more than they help. E-mail, in particular, lends itself to the creation of an ongoing written record so that partners can look back and confirm specific agreements or validate specific reports. E-mail also provides the opportunity to copy others simultaneously, a feature that can be used to the child's advantage (as when Big Brother is watching) or to the adult's advantage (as when an attorney receives copies).

   Anyone using these media must be aware that privacy loses its meaning. Each of these digital media is vulnerable to electronic eavesdropping and interception. In a twist on the famous deception scripted in Rostand's 1897 play, *Cyrano de Bergerac*, parents have been known to let their new partners, neighbors, friends, and, in one memorable case, even a hired child psychologist, ghostwrite their co-parenting communications in the interest of winning praise for their astute parenting rather than meeting their children's needs.

5. *Time-delayed spoken and written messages* can help conflicted parents put aside their emotions in the interest of providing better-organized, more constructive, and child-centered communications. Co-parents might agree, for example, to communicate all nonurgent matters by leaving one another messages on home or cell answering services or in writing via the postal service.

Voice messages and letters that are written out can be archived for future reference (keeping in mind that writers should always maintain copies of their communications), but are also easily intercepted by curious children and nosy visitors.

6. *A co-parents' notebook?* Both real-time and time-delayed written communications have the additional advantage of lending themselves to consistent structure. In one common format, co-parents agree that the sending parent will write out an update about the kids using a prearranged format so that the receiving parent will be up to date with the kids' needs as soon as possible upon arrival. This technique can help to script the kids' transition between caregivers.

Although the details of any such structured communication format will need to be specific to the child's needs and circumstance, one such format is provided on the following page as a sample.

A format like this one can be printed onto a page, copied 100 times, and bound in a ring binder. In this medium, the sending parent completes one column for each child just before the transition. The completed notebook is then delivered from one adult hand directly to another at the transition.

When handled in an e-mail format, the categories from this worksheet are used as headers for each child's update and sent within the hours before transition so that the receiving parent has the opportunity to be relatively current at the time of transition ("Hey, Billy. I heard that you got a home run last night!").

Sending parent: _____ Date/Time: _____	Child: _____	Child: _____
Eating/Appetite **Sleeping** **Toileting**		
Physical Health (Growth, injury, illness, medication, vision, hearing, appointments, and concerns)		
Academics (Class work and homework, grades, tests, quizzes, projects, plans, and events; special education update)		
Behavior (Compliance with authority, changes, habits, rewards, privileges, and punishments)		
Child's Successes **Accomplishments** **Matters of Pride**		

In either medium, the rules are the same: the kids never have access to the co-parenting notebook. Updates are written as concise, bulleted items. No prose. No explanations. Anything that requires explanation is either urgent and deserving of a more immediate communication or is better explained by the child

("Yeah, I tried that two-handed grip on the bat that you taught me, and it really worked!"). The co-parenting notebook never contains adult comments or financial information, as these call for a different medium of expression.

7. *Web-based communications* can provide co-parents a non-confrontational, confidential (at least to the extent that a password-protected website can be considered confidential), comprehensive, and minimally intrusive means of keeping current on the kids. Rather than receiving an e-mail, IM, text message, or conventional letter, a web-based service allows a parent to record relevant information and leave it to be picked up by an inquiring co-parent. Therapists, physicians, and other concerned adults can be given access for similar purposes.

   There are a number of such web-based services, including family calendars available on www.yahoo.com and www. google.com, and more elaborate, subscription services such as www.scheduleus.com and www.ourfamilywizard.com.

8. *Communicating through an intermediary* is the last and usually the least desirable among these options. When one or both co-parents feel threatened by their partner's words and cannot manage even a scripted, written exchange, all that remains may be communication through attorneys or a mediator. In this unfortunately familiar dynamic, Mom wants to know if she can take Billy to the beach for the upcoming long weekend but, unable to contact Dad directly, she calls her lawyer's office. A paralegal takes a message for the attorney. The attorney dictates a letter to his secretary, the letter reaches Dad's attorney's attention a full week later, who then consults with Dad. . . .

The benefit of this circuitous, inefficient, and very expensive process is that co-parents who would otherwise communicate nothing at all are able to exchange some very select and limited information. Above and beyond the obvious costs is the dependency that ensues. Co-parents who rely upon an intermediary often have no opportunity to lower their defenses and discover how else they might communicate in the future.

Big Brother Is Listening

With all due credit to George Orwell's then-futuristic novel, *1984*, it is a simple fact that most people behave more civilly and make choices more carefully when someone is looking over their shoulder.

Co-parent communication can benefit from this effect when parenting partners discuss their children's needs (a) in a public place or in the presence of a therapist or mediator, (b) with voice-to-voice conversations that conferences in a third party, or (c) by copying a neutral observer on written communications.

Big Brother can be a particularly effective technique when co-parents communicate via e-mail. A co-parenting facilitator, couples' therapist, guardian ad litem, or parenting coordinator can be copied on these communications simply using the message's cc: line. Then the parents are held accountable for their communications.

"Urgent" Matters

No one ever expects an emergency. Few of us even want to think about the possibilities, but healthy co-parents need to be prepared for every contingency. A serious car accident or injury, a house fire or theft, an abrupt illness, a self-destructive gesture, a drug- or alcohol-related incident, school suspension or expulsion—unfortunately, the list of potential crises is very long and not at all specific to children of a certain age or gender, or economic or geographic situation.

For all but the most extremely conflicted co-parents, a child's emergency is reason to throw standard operating procedure out the window. A co-parenting notebook or web-based communication medium may be wonderfully useful for routine matters, but is not the place to learn that your child is in the hospital. Once the danger is under control, caregivers have a responsibility to alert one another directly, succinctly, and constructively to the situation at hand. This generally means a phone call.

In some situations co-parents are legally and explicitly prohibited from phoning one another. Restraining orders, for example, limit specific forms of contact. If any such legal restraint is relevant to your co-parenting situation, call your attorney or the court today. Ask whether communicating directly with your co-parent in case of an emergency breaches the legal restriction and, if so, what contingencies can be established now, just in case.

If there is no such restriction on your co-parenting communication, reach your co-parent to plan ahead: "What should we do if there's an emergency while Billy is with one of us?" Is there a 24/7/365 emergency cell number that can be called? Is there an emergency text message

("911") or voice message ("Emergency. Call back ASAP!") that will alert you to call immediately?

Unfortunately, co-parents who allow themselves to become caught up in a child's emergency without thinking about the child's need for the other parent, those who intentionally exclude a co-parent from responding to a crisis for selfish reasons, and those who aren't available or don't respond when an emergency occurs can do damage that resonates for years to come. It's always better to incorporate now a "what if?" crisis contingency into the parenting plan.

Co-Parent Emergency Preparedness

Emergency preparedness includes a co-parent communication plan and more. Recognizing that the child's health and well-being must always trump the adults' conflict, healthy co-parents should always help one another to have the following:

1. A way to reach the child's other parent at all times.
2. A copy of the child's health insurance information.
3. A copy of the child's birth certificate when traveling.
4. A copy of any relevant court order (assigning joint legal decision-making authority, for example).
5. Relevant professionals' (pediatrician, psychotherapist, for example) phone numbers.
6. Names and dosages of all medications and details about serious allergies, as well as physical, emotional, or cognitive impairments and limitations.

7. Written permission for a nonguardian caregiver (for example, stepmom) to make emergency medical decisions.

Other reasonable precautions, particularly when traveling, include assuring that the child has photo identification with her at all times, that she wears a medical alert bracelet or anklet as necessary, and that the local Child Find (1-800-I-AM-LOST or www.childfindofamerica.org) data are up to date.

Is There Such a Thing as Too Much Communication?

Yes. There is such a thing as too much communication.

It's too much when it's constant. Barring emergencies, separated co-parents seldom need to communicate more than once a day. Many co-parents manage with a single communication each week or each parenting period, whichever is briefer. A transition e-mail or handwritten notebook (see "Finding a Happy Medium" in this chapter) may be sufficient.

It's too much when it's intrusive. Co-parenting communications that edge beyond the kids' needs, interests, successes, and failures and into personal adult matters aren't necessary. That's not to say that co-parents can't or shouldn't share these things, simply that they don't belong in the co-parenting communication. The transition e-mail should be exclusively about the kids. The co-parents' notebook should be exclusively about the kids. The words exchanged face-to-face at the next transition should be exclusively about the kids. In particular, any written communication that might be collected and reviewed later should be about the kids and nothing more.

It's too much when it serves to keep you artificially connected. We must never use our children and our mutual responsibility as their caregivers as an excuse to maintain an adult relationship. Co-parenting communications must only ever serve the child's needs. If and when communicating about the child becomes the means to an adult end, it's too much. Under these circumstances, the adults need to work out their relationship far away from the children, maintaining their co-parenting communications uninterrupted all the while.

It's too much when it becomes harassing, abusive, intimidating, or otherwise destructive. Although you have a responsibility to always take the high road, to make every reasonable effort to keep your co-parent current and your children out of the middle, you have an equal (and sometimes opposite) obligation to your own health and safety. If communication with your co-parent puts you at risk, it's time to find a new medium for communication. A Big Brother–mediated communication may be helpful. A facilitated co-parenting intervention or a parenting coordinator may be necessary.

Chapter 14

How Children React

W e humans are an incredibly adaptable species. We have the physical and emotional (and in recent decades have developed the technological) tools to adjust to an astonishing variety of experiences and environments. There is no place on this planet that we have not yet traveled and almost no place that we cannot live. Our cultures have developed as many ways of creating and defining relationships as there are people to relate to.

And yet our children are more vulnerable than the children of most species. Our babies are born less physically mature and self-sufficient even than babies born to our primate cousins. Our children need us for a relatively longer period of nurturing and protection. They need more parenting. Fortunately, for all of their physical neediness, our children have the social and emotional adaptability of Play-Doh.

Separate identical twins at birth. Place Baby A with a boisterous, active, fun-loving parent. Place Baby B with a quiet, serious, introverted parent. The children will grow up quite differently, each developing a sense of self and a relationship style that fits in with their respective caregivers. They will look alike, but Baby A will be the class clown who disturbs Baby B's studying.

What Role Does Temperament Play?

This twin study is real and has been demonstrated over and over again.

Does this mean that environment determines everything? That there is no such thing as a genetic or biological predisposition?

In fact, we are each born with a personality predisposition called a temperament. Some of us are predisposed to be more active and curious and flexible while others tend to move slower, to be more cautious and more set in their ways. But temperament itself is malleable. It can be shaped, at least to some small degree. The drive to fit into our social environment is strong enough to bend even these genetic predispositions or break trying.

Unfortunately, child psychologists', vice principals', and pediatricians' offices, not to mention police stations and hospitals and park benches, are bursting at the seams with people who don't fit in—people who rebel and reject and lash out or withdraw in ways that concern and confuse their caregivers and society as a whole. With a few extreme exceptions, as children they likely struggled with the same essential drive that shaped you and me into who we are and how we each fit into our respective social environments. For one reason or another, these people adapted poorly, and society has relegated them to a variety of more or less effective fixes and punishments.

And so it goes with children whose caregivers are conflicted, separated, or divorced. Like the rest of the species, these kids bring a tremendous drive to fit in and an impressive capacity for adaptation to their childhood experience. Understanding how our kids adapt to our adult conflicts—how the experience of being caught in the middle can shape identity and relatedness—is a lesson every parent should learn.

Separation Anxiety and Transitional Objects

Temperament makes some children more like Hummers and some children more like hybrids. A Hummer is a very large, very heavy vehicle that gets very poor gas mileage. A hybrid is typically a smaller, lighter vehicle that combines technologies to go much farther on a gallon of gas. All other things being equal, a Hummer needs to get refueled much more often than a hybrid.

All other things being equal, some children need to be refueled—to feel a caregiver's nurturing presence—more often than others. Some children are Hummers. Some are hybrids.

You and your co-parents are the gas stations. Your kids will learn fairly quickly that they can get their physical needs taken care of in many places in many ways (a neighbor's kitchen, the school cafeteria), but there are very few ways to get emotionally refueled. From early on, they will shape their behavior to make sure they can keep their tanks full.

In the typical course of development, children work toward greater and greater separateness or autonomy. They move farther and farther away from their caregivers as time goes on. By six months of age, the infant's attention wanders around the environment from a caregiver's lap, taking in the variety of sights, sounds, tastes, and textures available, but always returning to look you in the eye, to be reassured that you're present—to refill their tiny little tanks.

As crawling and walking and running and school buses and driver's licenses gradually enter the picture, our kids move farther and farther away. The three-year-old toddles into the next room confident and proud until he looks around, discovers that you're not there, and cries out to be picked up, to be refueled. The seven-year-old rides her two-wheeler down the block until the bully scares her or she skins her knee and she comes running back to be bandaged and cuddled—to refill her emotional gas tank. The college freshman bops about from dorm to class to coffee shop until a crisis hits, and then he reaches out to reconnect with you for precisely the same reason: to be refueled.

The crisis that hits when the child has gone as far as he can and discovers that his tank is empty is called separation anxiety. Separation anxiety is the metaphorical frantic call to AAA: "Help, I'm stranded! Come refuel me!"

The Hummers among our kids come running back often. They're more prone to separation anxiety. Their tank needs to be refilled more frequently, and they burn more quickly through the fuel that you give them. The hybrids among our kids go farther, with separation anxiety hitting less often and less easily. They come back less often, and they make the nurturance that you give them last far longer.

Somewhere along the way, cognitive changes allow our children to stow an extra tank of gas in their trunks, just in case. They become intellectually and emotionally able to carry a piece of their caregivers around in their brains so that some stumbles and skinned knees and college crises can be managed without a trip back to the gas station. Separation anxiety hits, but it's under control. They become able to refuel themselves just a little, to go just a bit farther. And then farther and farther, until their fuel efficiency and their spare tank prove sufficient to manage almost anything.

That spare tank of nurturance is called a transitional object. It can be anything that represents you or your child's other caregiver and the emotional fuel that you together provide. Little ones have blankets and pacifiers and stuffed animals. Bigger kids have photos and lockets and lunchboxes.

When intimate adult relationships conflict and end, when co-parents move apart, children are often forced to cope with separations for which they might not otherwise be ready: long periods with one caregiver away from the other, or confusion about when and where and if and how they can get back to the other caregiver to get refueled.

In this situation, separation anxiety can blossom to the point that it is disabling. School attendance is affected. Other expressions of anxiety (including otherwise unexplained physical symptoms) run rampant. The child feels like she's driven off into totally unfamiliar terrain, that she's run out of gas and no one is answering her calls. The parent-on-duty is trying, but that's not the gas that she needs.

What to do?

Healthy co-parents are able to put aside their own needs to make certain that the child's needs are met first and foremost. This calls for parenting plans that are well-suited to the child's individual needs and communication that is responsive and flexible.

And healthy co-parents, aware of what their children need and how they grow, anticipate these crises in the same way that a long-distance driver plans out his pit stops, anticipating refueling needs and taking reasonable steps to see that his tank is never empty.

We do this by creating transitional objects.

A transitional object will be unique to your child's needs, but generally should be portable and pocketable. Your kids need to be able to have it with them and yet be able to put it aside when necessary.

A transitional object can communicate the absent caregiver's presence to the child through any sense. A visual (photo) or written (note) transitional object may be more useful (and even more acceptable) to older and more emotionally mature kids. A transitional object that communicates your presence through touch (fleece), smell (perfume), or taste (lip gloss) will be more effective with younger, less mature, and more deeply stressed kids.

A transitional object can be continuously available, as when Mom gives Billy her necklace to wear under his T-shirt while visiting with Dad, or it can be provided by the parent-on-duty as needed, as when Dad writes a dozen JIC (just-in-case) notes for Billy and leaves them with Mom.

A transitional object may need to be "refilled" the same way that a spare gas can, once used, can be refilled. If Dad, for example, sleeps in an old T-shirt for three nights in a row and sends it with Sally to wear as her nightshirt when she's at Mom's house, Dad's scent will have dissipated by the time Sally returns a week later. In this case, Dad simply reclaims the T-shirt for several nights until the T-shirt once again communicates his presence to Sally while they are apart.

Today's technology lends itself to creating a variety of multimedia transitional objects, acknowledging that these often stretch portability and pocketability standards. A photo taped inside a lunch box or a JIC video of a happy time together with the absent caregiver can become powerful means of refueling. A parent who records bedtime stories several nights in succession back-to-back-to-back can help a child fall asleep in her other house listening to her familiar voice.

Transitional Object Dependence?

"But her transitional objects are interfering with our relationship!"

Some parents complain that their kids overuse their blanket or pacifier or the video that the absent parent sent over. The concern is that by relying on the transitional object, the child misses out on opportunities to develop another relationship and to otherwise have fun.

Although this can be the case in some rare instances, the child who clings this desperately to her transitional object is communicating something about her fragile emotional state. Rather than take this behavior personally, rather than becoming defensive ("She hates me!") or blaming ("Her father put her up to this!"), start by looking at what this behavior means about the child. Is she worried about the absent parent, fearing that something will happen while they're apart? Is she scared or otherwise anxious with the parent-on-duty, clutching the transitional object like a life preserver in a flood?

Patience is always the first, best strategy. She's more likely to give up the transitional object in a patient, understanding, and nurturing environment as she grows more comfortable than in a pressured and demanding environment.

Understanding the emotions that you bring to this situation is also critically important. Is your anger at your former intimate partner interfering with your ability to let your child feel good about him? Does her transitional object represent an unwelcome intrusion into your home? In either case, sorting through your priorities is necessary. Her needs must always trump yours.

Talking this concern out with your co-parent is probably the next best step. Perhaps you'll discover that your child clings to transitional objects connecting her to you in her other home, suggesting powerful emotions associated with reunion fantasies.

If these fail, consulting with the child's pediatrician or a child-centered mental health professional may then be a reasonable step. An objective third-party perspective can often help concerned and conflicted co-parents see the situation in a new light and discover new and healthier responses.

One rule of thumb is woven through all of this: a transitional object is not just another toy in your child's vast collection of stuff. It is a critical part of her fragile sense of security and well-being. As such, it is seldom a good idea to use it as incentive ("If you make your bed you can have your binky") or as punishment ("You didn't eat your supper so no binky for you!").

Your Kids' Expectations

Children who experience their parents' conflicts, separation, and/or divorce share a number of common beliefs long after the actual events have passed. These hopes and fears, wishes and dreams are entirely illogical and irrational. They defy factual reality, which prompts many parents to say, "No, he doesn't feel that way!"

But he does and they do, so we must start understanding how our kids feel, how they adapt, and what they expect. Only then can we hope to keep them out of the middle.

1. *Your children will have many conflicted and powerful feelings.* Don't fall for the steely faced denials or the distracted "I don't care" or even "I'm happy you guys are finally apart." When parents separate, children go through a grief process. We know that grief creates a confusing collage of emotions, from relief and happiness through anger, fear, and sadness.

2. *We must expect and allow our kids to experience the full range of healthy emotions for as long as they need, keeping our own powerful (grieving) feelings out of it and always clear about how strong feelings can be appropriately expressed.* "It's okay to be mad," you might say, "but we always expect you to be polite and respectful." On this latter note, remember that you must practice what you preach: how do you express your strong feelings?

3. *Your child will respond in a black-and-white way.* Young children see the world in all or nothing, black-and-white terms. Older children develop the capacity to see gray in between, but are vulnerable to regress back to a more simplistic view when stressed. For this reason, kids are prone to see one parent as good and the other as bad. This view is destructive to the extent that it is inaccurate, and it gets in the way of the child's ability to maintain a

healthy relationship with both parents. Unfortunately, an immature parent can easily confirm this primitive distinction for selfish
reasons and do profound damage to the child in the process.

4. *Your child will blame himself.* The logical, indisputable evidence
   to the contrary might be written on billboards across the county,
   but this probably won't dent your child's belief. He will blame
   himself in some way at some time for the adult conflict. Tragically
   often, this misbelief does rest on at least a grain of reality. The
   arguments were about him: how the two of you responded to his
   behavior, how his very existence complicates your life, how the
   two of you had been fine before he was born. Tragically, the result
   can be a child who blames himself for being born and, worse still,
   a child who runs away or becomes self-destructive in the belief
   that if he weren't around, his parents would be fine.

   Beware that in trying to relieve your kids of their self-blame,
   you don't redirect their anger onto yourself or their other parent.
   Rather than, "It's not your fault, Billy. It's all my fault!" work out a
   "we" statement that makes the separation an adult matter.

5. *Your child will wish for (and may try to engineer) a reconcili-
   ation.* Adults whose parents divorced decades earlier often admit
   to a lingering wish for their parents' reunion. Movies like *Parent
   Trap* only fuel the fire. Beware of the real "parent trap" here: the
   child who comes to you, eyes full of tears, and asks whether you
   and her mom are getting back together is setting you up to make
   a promise you can't keep. Best to start by responding to the emotion she's expressing rather than the content of the question,
   "You're really sad about these changes, aren't you?"

6. *Your child will expect (and may try to precipitate) rejection.* A child who sees the love between his caregivers end may believe that your love for him can end as well. This is most graphically illustrated by the child who is told, "Your dad and I got angry at each other, so we got divorced," and thereafter fears his own anger. Because it is human nature to poke at the weak spots in our safety nets (part of the reason that you probably drive five or ten miles per hour over the speed limit), the same child might also become very angry, testing how far he can go before he too gets rejected.

7. *Your child will try take advantage of the situation.* He'll try to guilt you into a later bedtime and ordering in pizza and buying him presents. He'll try to split between you and his other parent, claiming, "Mommy let's me. Why don't you?" He'll tell each parent that he's at the other parent's home when, in fact, he's out with his friends. When any of these manipulations succeed, you might see a huge smile of gratitude and glee. What you won't see immediately is the seed of insecurity that's been planted because the structures meant to hold him have failed.

Migrant Children: When Kids Stop Being Kids

We talk a lot about divorce in the United States, but much too little about one of its most obvious effects. The epidemic of co-parental conflict, separation, and divorce that characterizes our society means that we are raising a generation of migrant children—a culture of go-between kids.

More and more children spend a majority—and for some, the entirety—of their lives shuttling back and forth between caregivers. One week with Dad, one week with Mom, then back again. It's like these kids are spending the even-numbered days in the green house, and the odd-numbered days in the red house, counting out weekends like pocket change—his, hers, his—simply to determine which parent to ask about attending a friend's birthday party, and carrying all of their essential belongings in a single bag like a refugee.

But refugees and the children of conventional migrant workers, kids who relocate from one place to the next because of a parent's job, and even those kids who split their time between a summer home and a winter home, generally move *with* their parents. The physical relocation and its associated loss of familiarity, friendships, and school continuity certainly can be traumatic, but these children have a single, constant emotional anchor.

They have new walls, a new room, and new neighbors but the same parents.

These other migrant children—the victims of their parents' conflicts—routinely move *between* parents. They live in a revolving door of constant separation and reunion, over and over again, waking up each day wondering which home they're in, which rules apply, how long it will be until the next transition, and how best to fit in.

If you've never lived this way, you probably can't understand the emotions. Long-haul truckers and jet-setting businesspeople travel a lot, but it's not the same. We're adults. We have better coping skills.

If you're a professional who splits work weeks between two distant offices, you might understand the confusion and disorganization that these kids live with, never sure if what you need is here or there. But that's why we have administrative assistants and PDAs.

If you are adopted, perhaps you understand the emotional turmoil that can accompany shifting emotional anchors, giving up one parent for another, but not the constant back-and-forth of it. If you have lost a parent, you likely understand the grief, but grief can end, and then you have the opportunity to move on.

The migrant child of conflicted caregivers has a unique human experience. She lives a grief that is constantly renewed. She must learn to adapt to her caregiving environments—to win each parent's love—as best as she can. Fortunately, most manage this feat quite well, maturing into healthy adults and learning to become healthy parents themselves.

Some others, however, find that a parent's love requires filling a role or adopting a belief even though we know that love should never be assigned a cost. These unhealthy relationships threaten our children's health and well-being, but the problem does not reside within the children. They do not suffer from a syndrome or a diagnosable illness. They are adapting to an unhealthy dynamic. They have been coerced by an unhealthy caregiver into compromising their childhoods.

Five such dysfunctional and destructive relationship dynamics are described in the sections that follow. These are the dynamics of adultification, parentification, and infantilization, and the dilemmas of the chameleon child and the alienated child. These each are highlighted here so that we, as healthy parents, can work to avoid them and, when necessary, begin to recognize and respond to them. But this must not be mistaken as a catalog of childhood illnesses or diagnoses. To communicate that the child is ill risks compounding the problem and even enabling one or more unhealthy caregiving behaviors.

If these dynamics must be characterized as illnesses, then the illness exists in the relationships. Treatment may be necessary, but treating the child or the parent will never be sufficient and might actually do more harm. When the problem is the dynamic between people, the patient is the relationship itself, and the cure can only occur when the relationship is changed.

The Adultified Child

The end of an intimate adult relationship understandably hurts. It can leave one or both adults needy, sad, angry, scared, or all of these things. Blinded by a tempest of emotions, overwhelmed by questions about beds and boxes and bank accounts, threatened by the prospect of litigation, it is unfortunately easy to accept support where it doesn't belong.

Kids are barometers of their caregivers' emotions. No matter how busy or distracted or uncaring they may seem, they know when we're hurting. A child who responds to a parent's pain with compassion is demonstrating impressive maturity, empathy, selflessness, and love. But a child's very kind and well-meaning offer of caring must never be accepted. "Thanks, sweetie," you say between the tears. "I'll be fine. Let's get your homework started."

Caregiving must always roll downhill, from parent to child. To reverse this direction, even briefly, to turn to your child for caring, love, and support is to adultify him, to artificially and prematurely promote the child into a peer or even a partner.

It's easy to say, "You're the man of the house, now," or "You and I are partners," or "We're roommates. You've got to carry your weight."

You talk over supper about his day in school and what you did while he was at Dad's. You're bursting to tell someone—you've been so lonely and sad recently—so you tell him about the date that you went on last night—what you did, where you went, how much you like your new friend, and how different he is from Dad. You might not even realize that you're talking with your child the same way that you'd talk with your best friend, the same way that you used to talk with your former partner—his other parent—in the good old days.

And he's listening. He's asking good questions. He isn't upset at all! Isn't that proof that he's mature enough to handle adult matters? That you can turn to him like this?

No. It's not. Don't do it.

You're letting your needs trump your child's needs. You're asking your child to take care of you. Of course he's listening. You've forgotten that your attention and affection are the fuel that keeps him going. If becoming your new confidant and best friend and replacing his other parent in your life is the way to win those precious commodities, then that's what he'll become.

He's being adultified, made into a peer in the interest of meeting your needs. He may think it's pretty cool to be treated like a grown-up, but he will also be scared and confused and feel very disloyal to his other parent by becoming your ally. He doesn't really understand all the things that you tell him (even though he fakes it pretty well), and he certainly isn't emotionally ready to cope with this new role.

Anxiety and Development

Among the many children who fill psychologists' offices seeking relief from disabling anxieties (intense phobias, school refusal, or obsessive-compulsive disorder, as examples), it's possible to identify a distinct minority with specific characteristics. These children are very intelligent but socially and emotionally only average. They are cognitively able to understand much more than they are emotionally able to handle. The result can take the form of intense anxiety.

As often as this developmental disparity spontaneously occurs (and may spontaneously remit as coping abilities catch up with intellectual ability), it can be artificially induced very easily.

A child who is invited into the adult world prematurely is exposed to much more than she is emotionally prepared to digest. She may grin and smile and ask for more, but she's faking it. She's fulfilling a role that a selfish adult has assigned to her as best as she's able. Her inability to genuinely cope with her new experience will show up somewhere, somehow: sleep difficulties, eating difficulties, unexplained physical symptoms, and anxiety.

The adultified child pays for his new role as Mom or Dad's best friend in childhood experiences lost—giving up same-aged friendships in favor of hanging out with his new best friend, missing out on activities and opportunities because Mom or Dad needs him, cheating himself out of the fantasies and fun that he should have and needs because "that's just kid stuff."

The best answer to the dilemma of the adultified child is to give her back her childhood. Allow her to move back from friend to daughter, from peer and partner back to child.

And what if your co-parent is adultifying your child? What if your child arrives in your home acting as if he's your friend or colleague and expecting to be treated the same, telling you stories about how his other parent gives him adultlike privileges? Be clear and firm about the roles and expectations in your home without demeaning anyone else's behavior and later, away from the kids, talk to your co-parent, never blaming him or her and never being hostile.

"Hey, here's what Sally's been saying . . . ," you wonder aloud, without blaming. "Can you fill me in?"

The Parentified Child

A child who is parentified fills a different niche than the adultified child in one or both homes.

Overwhelmed and needy, torn by emotions, and struggling to make ends meet, you've unexpectedly found yourself raising two or more children unassisted. The person you depended upon as your intimate partner and co-parent is gone. The adult relationship is over. Now you're up at dawn feeding the baby, dropping one at day care and two at school before you get to work late, where you're swamped and mistreated and earn way too little for eight hours, just in time to reverse the trip and finally get home to make supper, do homework, clean the house, do the laundry, and try to pay the bills.

Your experiment making time by giving up eating and sleeping isn't going so well. You can't afford more child care or help with the housework, and your friends offer, but you know this is a bottomless pit that needs enormously more than they could do or you would ever ask for, so . . . bit by bit you ask more of your oldest. Change the baby. Warm the formula. Toast the breakfast. Pack the lunch boxes.

"Just sit with her till she falls asleep this one time while I throw a load of laundry in, okay?"

Just like the adultified child, the parentified child has been prematurely promoted into an adult role. The need is genuine. This situation is a crisis that may be unmanageable and even harmful in a dozen other ways. Parentifying the oldest makes sense there and then. But it comes with a cost.

Above and beyond the childhood experiences lost and the opportunities missed, the parentified child is at risk for defining herself forever more as a nurturer. She develops relationships with needy partners and nurtures them. She has children and gives and gives and gives some more until, sometime in her adulthood, she finds herself empty and unfulfilled. She is a nurturer who is unable to accept nurturance. She is angry at all of the people in her life who are unable to give to her, and she is angry at herself for maintaining relationships that drain her dry.

In some instances, the child who is parentified goes on to become an empty, needy, and resentful parent herself. Knowing no better, she repeats the damaging role reversal by seeking nurturance from her own child, and on and on, across generations of children nurturing their parents.

How does it stop? Sometimes it doesn't. And other times it stops because a mother who was parentified as a child miraculously finds the inner strength to be a healthy parent to her own child. This strength is among the most beautiful and astonishing gifts that any parent can give.

The Infantilized Child

Everyone needs to feel needed, valued, and important to others.

As adults, we typically develop relationships that meet this need, that make us feel needed—with colleagues and peers at work, neighbors and friends, extended family, the members of the bowling league, the ladies in the church group, and even our pets. Each of these relationships might create a slightly different sense of personal value and importance that together fill our need to feel needed.

Parenthood can constrict an adult's world dramatically, particularly when your intimate adult partner and would-be co-parent is missing in action or abusive. Throw some anxiety and depression into the mix, and it's easy to find yourself spending all of your time alone with your baby. The result is an adult who fulfills her need to feel needed through her child.

This can work through the long and amazing months of infancy and into the child's toddler years without necessarily harming anyone. The problem appears later, as the child reaches toward greater and greater independence but the parent cannot let go. This parent has herself become dependent on the child's dependence and neediness. She selfishly needs him to remain a clingy little baby, so she more or less subtly and even unconsciously punishes his independence. She withdraws her attention when he takes his first steps. She cries when he expresses an interest in preschool. She becomes morose and depressed when he develops friendships away from her. And she floods his least mature, most regressed behaviors with the rewards of her doting attention and affection.

This parent might not see the dynamic that she's created. She may be confused about the child's developmental delay and concerned about his resistance to separating from her, but she quietly reaps the benefit of these dynamics by feeling needed. This is infantilization, a relationship dynamic that reinforces a child's immature, regressed, and even infantile dependence for the sake of a very needy adult.

Outside of this dysfunctional relationship—at school, with friends, or in the other parent's care—the child might seem unremarkable, a little immature, perhaps, but nothing startling until she returns to the infantilizing parent's care. In this environment, her independence quickly withers and dies. Toileting skills are lost, and mature expressive skills are compromised. Baby talk emerges, and she clings.

The Pathologized Child

In some very disturbed and relatively rare instances of infantilization, a parent's need to be needed reaches the extreme of inducing illness in the child. This has been known variously as Munchausen disease by proxy and, more recently, as a type of factitious disorder.

This pathological and very dangerous dynamic requires the immediate intervention of a multidisciplinary team of child-centered professionals first to determine that the child is not ill or that her illness has been artificially induced and subsequently to address the dynamics that have fostered this situation. In many instances, the child cannot recover from the induced or exacerbated illness unless and until her residential care and her contact with the inducing caregiver have been radically altered.

Beware that a child whose behavior is significantly less mature than that of his age mates is not necessarily infantilized. Child-centered medical and mental health professionals must be involved in order to rule out the three other most likely suspects: stress-related regression, developmental differences, and cognitive delay.

Stress-related regression refers to the normal and expectable loss of mature skills in response to extreme and prolonged stress. In some cases, co-parental conflict, separation, and divorce can induce regression, causing a child to back down the developmental staircase. Toileting problems, baby talk, or clinginess may resume, but only briefly. As the stress subsides, healthy development will resume.

Developmental differences and cognitive delays can cause a child to appear less mature than her age mates. Diagnosable difficulties including pervasive developmental disorder (PDD), autism, certain rare genetic difficulties, and mental retardation must be evaluated and considered as possible causes by skilled professionals. Unlike the infantilized child whose maturity may vary dramatically from one environment to another, children struggling with any of these other causes of immaturity will behave uniformly across environments.

The Chameleon Child

Perhaps the best way to adapt to a life that is split between two very different environments is to blend into each, chameleon-like. The chameleon child does exactly this and, in so doing, may be the most difficult to identify among children with these unhealthy adaptive strategies.

The chameleon child does and says exactly what is necessary to fit into Dad's home and then, just a short car ride later, does and says exactly what is necessary to fit into his mother's home. In one parent's company he's green, and in the other's company he's blue. He seldom stands out or causes a fuss or draws attention to himself. His goal is to fit in, to keep the peace. He seems like an ideal child, never mind that he is compromising his identity in the process.

The chameleon child is a balloon waiting to burst. He is swallowing his ideas and opinions and feelings in the interest of keeping the peace. Having seen conflict destroy love, he implicitly believes that if he were to stir up conflict he would not be loved. He may fear anger most of all, hiding his own anger within himself in the short term because no other expression is acceptable. In the long term, of course, the balloon will burst. The accumulated rage will either implode in depression and self-destructive choices or explode in a fury that can reach the level of violence.

Parents who enroll their chameleon child in individual psychotherapy (usually for an incidental concern, like declining school grades) seldom complete the therapy. They routinely complain that the child is getting worse, that he's becoming defiant and oppositional, and that he no longer fits in. Of course! The chameleon child, like his adultified and parentified and infantilized and alienated peers, has adapted to an unhealthy environment. He will not change until the environment that fosters his unhealthy behavior changes. The chameleon child's parents must learn to tolerate and even to encourage their child's emerging identity and all of the powerful thoughts and feelings that go with it.

The Alienated Child

Alienation is certainly the most well-known among these several adaptive dynamics. Unfortunately, the word itself has become supercharged with controversy. Mental health and family law professionals argue about it in writing and debate about it at meetings. Conflicted co-parents invest their lives and their savings in litigation over it. As such, any single definition must be understood as a point of contention, at least, and will be found by some to be simply inflammatory.

Alienation is a natural and necessary dynamic as old and as useful as the concept of the family group. Alienation and its counterpart, the dynamic of alignment, are together the tools of affiliation. These are the tools that groups use to define who is "in" and who is "out" and, in the process, help members define their identity through association.

In the context of family, alienation occurs when a caregiver provides a child with information that causes the child to become less secure about another person. As a healthy and necessary tool, parents say things like, "Don't talk to strangers," or "Stay away from Mr. Smith. He's creepy." These alienating messages define who is outside of the family group and instill in the child anxiety intended to keep him safe.

Alignment is the flip side of the same coin. Alignment occurs when a parent provides a child with information that causes the child to feel more secure with another person. Statements such as, "You've got a great teacher," or "Talk to your counselor," serve this purpose.

Groups commonly use the tools of alienation and alignment in order to define membership and enhance healthy competition. Members of sporting teams build one another up but deride their opponents.

Salespeople sing their colleagues' praises and proclaim their competitors' failings. Flags and uniforms and mottos define who is in through alignment. Graffiti, election-year political advertisements, insults, and jeers define who is out through alienation.

Teenagers depend upon these same tools as they move away from family toward greater autonomy. They align with clubs, organizations, churches, cliques, frats, and gangs, wearing the right colors and knowing the right password and using the secret handshake.

Like any tool, these dynamics can also be used as weapons. When an unhealthy or malicious father exposes his daughter to his anger at her mother, he risks contaminating the child's security with her mother. When the message is loud enough and long enough and when the child's security with the mother is already weak enough, the damage is done. The child will begin to feel unsafe in her mother's care. She may begin to resist or refuse spending time with her. Co-parental alienation has occurred.

As in the instances of adultification, parentification, infantilization, and the chameleon child, it is important to understand that alienation is not a syndrome or a diagnosable illness. It does not reside within the child, but exists and persists as a function of the child's continuing relationships. Although the best remedies for co-parental alienation are still as controversial as the dynamic itself, it is clear that there can be no medication or surgery or individual intervention. Psychotherapy with the child alone, for example, can never be sufficient. Only the intervention or suite of interventions that changes the entire relationship dynamic—including both the alienating caregiver's communications and the targeted parent's behavior—can ever hope to be successful.

Can Co-Parent Alienation Be Necessary and Appropriate?

Sadly, the answer to the above question is yes. It's known as estrangement.

In the same way that a parent's efforts to induce a child's insecurity with strangers is sound and defensible, there must be occasions when a parent's efforts to induce a child's insecurity in a co-parent who is known to be abusive or neglectful are similarly so.

For example, when intimate adult partners separate because Mom is volatile and violent, Dad is arguably making a healthy choice when he cautions his kids to be careful while they're with their mother. He might prompt before a transition, "Do you have your cell phone?" and "Remember how to dial 911?" and "You can always go to the next-door neighbors if you feel scared." The kids may be physically safer, but they've been put right in the middle. Their relationship with their mother may be contaminated by their father's words.

Their emotional safety net is shredded in the interest of their physical safety.

The better choice? When a co-parent is objectively violent and volatile, abusive or neglectful, it will always be a better choice to establish adult protections than to ask the kids to protect themselves. This may mean restraining orders or supervised or therapeutic visitation. With these protections in place, the kids can visit with their other parent without any need for estrangement.

Chapter 15

What's an Overwhelmed Co-Parent Supposed to Do?

Your emotions are raw. It's been a roller coaster of ups and downs. Maybe the planets are misaligned or your biorhythms are out of sync. Maybe you need to floss more often or give up caffeine. Whatever the reason, it's really hit the fan.

Your intimate adult relationship is falling apart. You can't stand the idea of spending another day with the partner with whom you once thought you'd spend the rest of your life. Work is miserable. The bills are overdue. Your therapist is on vacation, your meds don't seem to be helping, and the toilet is clogged!

As if all of that weren't bad enough, the one person who makes it all worthwhile, your precious child, is treating you like garbage. Where did that cute little kid go? Doesn't it matter that you're working your bottom off to put food on the table and batteries in his gizmos? Whatever happened to gratitude?

"If I'd treated my mom or dad the way that he's treating me, I would have gotten a good smackeroo . . ."

Stop right there. A generation ago and beyond, back into the times when children were possessions to be seen and not heard, parents used violence to curb children's misbehavior. And it worked! A child who discovered that a specific behavior resulted in a hit from Mom or Dad learned very quickly not to repeat that behavior. The problem is that he also learned to be scared of his parents and to use violence to get his own way. Getting hit may have scared him out of a behavior, but he never learned a different, more acceptable choice in its place.

Is that what's wrong with our society? We've become softies? Should we go back to hitting our kids?

Absolutely not. Violence has no place in parenting. Don't let the fact that a number of states still allow corporal punishment lead you to believe that it's a reasonable behavior management strategy. It's not. Changing behavior through pain, intimidation, and humiliation is not parenting; it's domination.

But there you are, at the end of your rope. It seems that the world is falling apart. You're exhausted, and your son or daughter is being rude and disrespectful—maybe even calling you names or ignoring you completely. Not so long ago, you could have tagged your co-parent into the ring and taken a break to refuel. But that's circular, because if you still had a relationship like that, you wouldn't be so on edge in the first place (and perhaps your kids wouldn't, either).

What's an overwhelmed parent supposed to do?

You're not thinking clearly (and no one ever does under these circumstances), so let's keep it simple:

1. *Don't hit.* Violence is never a successful tool for learning.
2. *Get safe.* If there is an immediate safety issue, take care of it now.

If the stove is on, turn it off. If you're driving, pull over safely. If you need immediate support because you feel like you might hurt yourself or someone else, or your child is threatening to hurt himself or someone else or to run away, dial 911 now or get to the hospital emergency room.

Once everyone is safe:

3. *Walk away.* Your emotions have taken charge. Your brain has shut down. You need to get out of the situation, even if only for five minutes. Go outside and breathe fresh air. Have a cold drink, but no alcohol and no over-the-counter or street drugs. If your physician recommends medication for times like this, follow doctor's orders.

4. *Don't join the battle.* Yes, your child's button-pushing, provocative, demanding, and demeaning behaviors are completely unacceptable. But as the parent you must see beyond the invitation to do battle, the white-glove-across-the-face challenge to duel. It can't matter that he's drawn a line in the sand, that he's *nah-nah, nah-nah-nah* taunting you, arms folded across his chest, thumbing his nose. Don't do it! As soon as you lower yourself to his level to respond to the challenge, all is lost. It doesn't matter who is stronger or who knows more swear words or who can make the other one cry first. Once you take the bait, everyone loses.

So what's a healthy parent supposed to do?

Firm, Calm, and Consistent

Make that phrase your co-parenting motto and your caregiving mantra: *Firm, calm, and consistent. Firm, calm, and consistent.* Say it over and over again to yourself, to your parenting partner, even to your kids.

Firm, calm, and consistent.

Firm, calm, and consistent.

Easier said than done, right?

Right. Even so, this is the only healthy way through these hard times. It is only by remaining firm, calm, and consistent that you can hope to anchor your kids in the midst of the storm. Other parenting responses might shut them down and shut them up, might get you through the moment or help you win the battle, but the war will rage on. The next battle will be sooner and bigger, and your responses will have to be louder and harsher, and no one will win. Everyone will lose.

Firm, calm, and consistent.

Firm, calm, and consistent.

Firm is the tone of your voice, your posture, and your eye contact. Firm is not angry. It's not intimidating. It's not threatening or menacing or bullying. Firm is confident and in-charge without bragging about it. Firm is usually not loud. In fact, you may find that a quiet voice—even a whisper—gets more attention and respect than anything ever screamed in the midst of an I-can-yell-louder-than-you battle.

Firm means sitting or standing erect, back straight, and communicating that you're serious. But be careful not to intimidate. Firm is communicated best at the same height as your child, even if this means stretching out on the floor.

And firm is about eye contact, but this one is tricky. Looking someone in the eye will often communicate a challenge. It can elicit a fight-or-flight response. Your goal is not intimidation. You're not looking for a fight, and you don't want your child to run away. Firm is sometimes communicated best when you're seated side-by-side, staring at or engaged in some common thing, not each other.

"Look at me, young man!" has its place. Easily distractible, ADHD-like kids lost in digital media are much more likely to realize that you're speaking, to register your words, and even to comply with your request, when you first establish eye contact. But in the context of an angry confrontation, "Look at me, young man!" is just another opportunity to do battle. It invites a power struggle that has nothing to do with the real issues and everything to do with domination and control. It's probably best not to go there.

Firm, calm, and consistent.

Calm is a constant goal. It may be as difficult as it is important to be calm in the face of all of the chaos and trauma in your life. Calm does not mean cold and emotionless. Your kids need to see that you have emotions (within reason) without being invited to take care of you. They need to learn from your example how to cope with and express strong emotions.

Calm means a deep cleansing breath, a quiet count to ten, and a silent reminder that you can scream later, when you're alone in the car, and that you can cry on your best friend's shoulder tomorrow at work. Calm means knowing that with your therapist or in your diary or back home in your own mother's arms you can rant about your kids and why your co-parent isn't there and how miserable life sometimes seems. Right now, calm means having the maturity and the emotional resources to lock all that fear, anger, sadness, and loneliness up in a box in your head and remember that your priority must be anchoring your kids.

Calm means anchoring yourself so you can anchor your children. Their emotions are already supercharged. If you add emotion to the exchange, their emotions will go out of control. If you are calm, they will be better able to rein themselves in, to calm themselves down as well.

And calm means that your words are conversational. The pace is neither anxious-rushed nor threatening-slow. The tone is neither hysterical-high nor James Earl Jones–deep. The words that you choose are neither psychobabble-sophisticated nor baby talk–condescending. Calm means brief, declarative statements using simple words.

"This discussion is over." Pause. Cleansing breath. "I will not be treated with disrespect. I will not disrespect you." Pause. Cleansing breath. "When you're able to talk to me respectfully, I'll be in the kitchen."

Firm, calm, and consistent.

Consistent? Consistent is about structure. Consistency is discussed in the Introduction section, "Structure Decreases Everyone's Anxiety." In this context, as in most, consistency means reassuring your children that their safety net is intact. The world remains predictable despite their rage and all the other changes swirling around them.

But consistent is especially difficult and important in this context. You're exhausted, sick, depressed, enraged, overwhelmed, and uncertain about everything in your life. Chances are that your child's invitation to do battle is fueled, at least in part, by your emotional turmoil. He's asking for reassurance, even though it sounds like name-calling, defiance, and disrespect.

Forcing Apologies

How important is that apology?

Some parents believe in demands that sound like, "Say you're sorry right now!" or "Apologize, young man!"

Sometimes these demands earn a timid and halfhearted, eyes downcast, "I'm sorry," but it's only a meaningless echo. "Say you're sorry right now!" invites another power struggle. If your child refuses, then you can argue about apologizing rather than about the real matter at hand. If your child gives in and echoes the words that you've demanded, it's empty. The real experiences of regret and remorse and requesting forgiveness are diluted and can become rote statements that are used to escape punishments and nothing more.

Probably the best way to teach your kids to say, "I'm sorry" is to be certain to apologize sincerely yourself when you regret your actions and to accept others' apologies just as sincerely.

It is all too easy in this situation to throw up your hands and say, "Do whatever you want, I don't care!" or "I'm calling your dad to come get you!" or "I can't take this anymore. I'm out of here!" or worse.

Don't. Take your overwhelmed, panicky, hopeless, helpless feelings elsewhere. He needs you right now. He needs you firm and calm and consistent. He needs the reassurance that the same rules and consequences and routines that have always applied still do. If you let your guilt, fear, rage, or depression change the rules, he might be thrilled ("I can stay up all night on a school night? Really? Thanks, Dad!") and you've sidestepped the battle for the moment, but it's not worth it in the long run. You've set a dangerous precedent ("But you let me last night!"), you've invited splitting ("But Mom let me!"), and worst of all, you've compromised the structure. You've torn a hole in the safety net. You've bought a moment's peace at the cost of your child's security.

When in Doubt, Go for the Feelings

Chapter 10 introduced the importance of responding to factual questions first by asking, "What do you think?" By contrast, when confronted by your child's powerful emotions, the first, best answer is to ask yourself, *What is she feeling?*

Our brains are only so big. The more that emotions fill them, the less room there is for thinking. When feelings are strong, logical decision making will be weak. Maturity fails. Regression occurs. Impulsive behaviors run rampant.

When feelings are strong, even the most rational and intelligent person can sound like a babbling idiot.

Confused or furious or terrified or grief-stricken or even joyous with pleasure and excitement, our thinking gets distorted, and we are all prone to say things that make no sense at all, that we will regret later, and that wound others whom we love.

Because you're the adult and you are practicing your mantra—*firm, calm, and consistent; firm, calm, and consistent*—you know not take your child's supercharged emotional statements at face value. You know not to take the bait. You know how to sidestep most of those invitations to do battle. And you know how important it is that you do these things.

But do you know the difference between the *content* and the *feelings* in a statement?

The content of a statement is the obvious part. It's probably about the noun ("I want a *toy*") or the verb ("Why can't I *go*?") in his complaint. When the content is about safety or is otherwise simple and obvious, then your response will be a firm, calm, and consistent statement. When she asks, for example, "Why can't I go to the bar? Sally is!" the content is simply about safety: "You're only fourteen. You may not go to the bar."

But when her question confuses you, makes the little hairs on the back of your neck stand up, or sparks a feeling in you, the content of the question comes second. The feelings in her question must come first. Start by labeling the emotion that she's expressing.

When Suzie screams "I don't want broccoli!" or "Give me back my car keys!" or "I can't believe that you're getting a divorce!" it's a mistake to start by responding about vegetables or driving or your marriage. You can do that later if it's still important. Right now, you recognize that her emotions are in charge, not her brain. She's not thinking clearly, so anything factual ("But broccoli contains vitamins . . .") is a waste of breath. It won't register. Better to start with, "Boy, I didn't know you had such strong feelings," or "You're really mad right now, huh?"

This is hard to do. It feels awkward and rarely comes naturally to most people. Our society has trained us to answer that two plus two equals four, not that two plus two can be a happy or sad or angry or fearful expression. But it can. And when it is, the answer "four" is next to worthless.

When she cries, "I don't want to go to Dad's anymore! I want to stay here!" do you respond about your needs and Dad's needs? About court orders or the GAL or contempt charges? No. You keep her out of the middle. You sidestep the supercharged content and lock away all of your feelings about her dad and your separation. You start by asking about the feelings ("I know that you're not happy, sweetie. Are you saying that you're sad or mad or scared?") or by labeling the obvious emotions ("This is pretty hard for you. You sound really nervous").

One warning: as important as it can be to sidestep the content in order to help your kids with their feelings, it is at least as important not to impose your feelings on them. To do this job right, you have to be able to step out of yourself—*firm, calm, and consistent*—and acknowledge her feelings, even if they contradict your own.

If you hear, "I don't know what to pack to take to Mom's this weekend," and respond with, "You're pretty scared of your dad, aren't you?" you'll get a confused look at best ("Huh? I was talking about clothes . . . ?") and at worst your chameleon kid (see Chapter 14) will agree immediately, even though she wasn't at all scared before you suggested it.

When Children Say "I Hate You!"

When an intimate adult relationship fails, the phrase "I hate you!" becomes a particularly powerful button for most adults. Beware that your kids will use it to test their safety net, but it probably doesn't mean what you first think.

"I hate you" between adults usually expresses the opposite of love. It's a destructive and angry declaration of wholly negative passion. More than the end of love, adults mean it as the antilove.

When children say the same words exactly, they usually mean something quite different. A child's expression of "I hate you!" usually means, "I'm mad at you!"

In the same way that we have to teach our kids that adult love is different from parent/child love, we must understand that adult "hate" usually means something completely different than a child's use of the word to a parent.

Do you know that anger is not the opposite of love? That happiness, sadness, anger, and fear are all experiences that can be part of a loving relationship? That each of these in the right context can actually enrich a loving relationship?

If you respond to a child's door-slamming scream of "I hate you!" with anything about love ("Well, I love you!" or—far worse—"Then I hate you, too!") you've missed the boat entirely. You've planted the seed that your love is finite and conditional, that your love can end.

Your daughter's declaration of "I hate you!" (and similar statements like, "I wish you were dead!" and "You're the worst parent in the world!" and "I only love Daddy, not you!") must be translated into grown-up as "I'm furious!" If you respond about her anger ("I know that you're really mad right now") you'll help her to better understand herself. Together you might then have a chance to talk about the real issue. Not about love, but about anger.

Validate, Don't Denigrate

Here is a common co-parenting challenge—one more test of your mature capacity to put your kids' needs first:

"I love Daddy more than you!"

Freeze frame. Let's think this through. What are your possible responses?

1. *"He's a jerk! How could you love him?"* No. Go back to page one. Do not pass go. Do not raise a healthy child. You are responding like an adult complaining to a peer about a failed relationship. You are the parent. You're speaking to your child. Your adult feelings have no place here. This response simply puts your child in the middle. In fact, you're doing worse. You may be adultifying or alienating her from her father.

2. *"If you love him, then you can't love me!"* No. This is the worst nightmare and the painful reality of too many children whose parents are conflicted. Keeping them out of the middle requires reassuring them that they can love you both despite the fact that you no longer love one another.

3. *"Why?"* No. This is not a factual statement that can be dissected and corrected like a problem in long division or an essay about the dinosaurs. To look for reasons misses the child's meaning and puts her in a situation to try to balance your self-proclaimed strengths against her other parent's strengths. Parent/child love is not a competition with a winner and a loser.

4. *"Here's ten reasons that you should love me more."* No. Put away your overintellectualized defensiveness. Later in this chapter,

you'll read more about avoiding defensiveness.

5. *"I'm glad that you love us both."* Better, but not great. You get brownie points for sidestepping the more/less competition implicit in her comment. Not great because the "I'm glad" preface puts your feelings into play. Certainly this should please you, but it's not about you, pleased or otherwise. It's about her feelings.

6. *"You can always love us both as much as you want."* Good. Give her permission. Deflate the competitiveness. Leave your feelings out of it. Acknowledge her emotion.

7. *"You certainly do have a terrific dad!"* Excellent. Validate her feelings. Validate her other parent's qualities. Sidestep the invitation to compete and the button-pushing *nah-nah, nah-nah-nah* nose-thumbing test of your confidence. Good work.

Now read on.

Never Defensive!

If you think that "firm, calm, and consistent" is tough, healthy co-parenting is about to get even tougher.

"Mom says that you're a jerk!"

Deep breath. Take five. Practice your mantra:

Firm, calm, and consistent.

Firm, calm, and consistent.

Is this a factual question that calls for a "What do you think?" response?

No. Of course not. It doesn't matter that you have fourteen college degrees and thirty-five personal references, that you belong to MENSA and won an Olympic gold medal in Lillehammer, all proving that you are not a jerk.

It certainly doesn't matter that you think if anyone's a jerk, it's your former partner—her other parent—or that you have videotape and court documents proving the point.

Defending yourself and—worse!—counterattacking with a tit-for-tat, quid-pro-quo insult puts your kids smack in the middle of the co-parent conflict. It asks them to take sides. It invites them to consider the evidence and choose one beloved caregiver over the other. Both are shortsighted and self-serving responses that neglect the children's needs entirely.

Don't go there.

While the words still hang in the air between you, it doesn't even matter that your former intimate partner used the same expletive to describe you last Friday at the child-care transition. Later, you might try to discover whether your child overheard that particular adult exchange and mimicked it and/or whether, perhaps, her other parent is talking to her about you in demeaning terms (see Chapter 14).

It may matter that her statement is boldly disrespectful. Whether you choose to respond to the way that the feeling is expressed depends on the parenting structures you have in place. If you've already established that speaking respectfully is a battle that you will fight (and particularly if the co-parenting team has agreed that respect is expected in both homes), then—in the interest of being firm, calm, and consistent—you might choose to respond to the way that she's expressing herself ("That language is unacceptable"). But be aware that there's a far bigger issue at hand.

What most matters, here and now, are her emotions. Not yours.

"Mom says that you're a jerk!" is an expression of feelings. The statement is disrespectful and provocative and pushes every button in your bruised and battered psyche, but it is ultimately all about her emotions. It's about her emotions. *Not* yours. You're firm, calm, and consistent. *Firm, calm, and consistent.*

"Mom says that you're a jerk!" is an important example because we all share a certain degree of reflex defensiveness which, unleashed, will only do harm. This is a maturity test for you—a challenge to see beyond the personal assault, to set aside your own ego, and to carefully separate the child's needs from your feelings about the adult who has hurt you. It's a test of your ability to remember that your child is not your peer and that she depends on you for her emotional well-being.

When you're able to look beyond the disrespectful and inflammatory words and beyond your own emotional turmoil, you'll begin to recognize her confusion ("It's hard when we argue so much, isn't it?") or her anger ("You sound really mad about that"), her resentment ("I'm really sorry that we've put you in the middle of this"), or her fear ("Don't worry, buddy, we're going to figure this out"). You'll remember to offer as much reassurance as possible using "we" statements and to always keep her out of the middle.

Chapter 16

When Children Resist
or Refuse Transition

W hen parents live apart, their children carry the burden of constantly transitioning between homes. This revolving-door cycle of change can be disruptive and distressing to all, but to no one more so than the kids themselves.

When a child resists or refuses to transition between caregivers, conflicted co-parents are left to judge whether this is just another power struggle in need of a firm, calm, and consistent response, or something larger. We can set firm limits and follow through with predictable consequences when a child refuses to go to bed, but should we do the same when he resists seeing his other parent?

It is unfortunately easy and all too common for the sending parent to see a child's transition resistance as validating his feelings about a former partner and the status of the intimate adult relationship. "She's lost me, and now she's losing her kids!" This is another form of conformational bias, the natural tendency that we all share to interpret ambiguity consistent with our existing beliefs (see Chapter 13). In the case of transition resistance and refusal, however, misreading the situation risks harming the child's relationship with one or both parents, on one hand, or unnecessarily exposing him to an unhealthy situation, on the other.

Four general rules are routinely helpful in resolving this dilemma:

1. *The more predictable and routine the transitions are, the better everyone will manage them.*

2. *Responding to a child's transition resistance or refusal sooner will always be better than later.* Like children who resist going to school, the longer they stay home ("Okay, we'll just let you skip today"), the harder it is to get them back on track. Your guilt and exhaustion, your wish to spend time with your child, and your anger at your co-parent have no place here.

3. *At the first sign of resistance, you and your co-parent have to talk it out.* This problem can only be successfully addressed by the co-parents as a team, aided, as necessary, by concerned others (the child's therapist, a mediator or parenting coordinator). An individual parent's unilateral efforts to respond to transition resistance will usually fail and often worsen the situation, no matter how well-intended.

4. *Transition resistance seldom occurs in response to a single factor.* Understanding the child's behavior and determining how best to respond to it calls for careful consideration of a number of factors that range from the benign and incidental to the more malignant and destructive.

Making Transitions Predictable

The first and easiest solution to a child's transition resistance and refusal is to increase structure. We know that structure decreases anxiety, and less anxiety means better functioning for everyone involved (review these ideas in the Introduction).

Increase the structure of the kids' transitions with the following ideas:

1. *Decrease the likelihood that face-to-face transitions between co-parents will erupt in conflict.* When your kids expect that the transition process will become just another opportunity to witness their caregivers' war, they'll transition about as easily as they go to the doctor's office to get a shot. Information about scripting in Chapter 9 can be helpful here.

2. *Increase the predictability of the transitions.* A parenting plan that sets up transitions at a single, predictable time will decrease anxiety and encourage compliance more than a schedule that juggles transitions across the week and throughout the day. Predictability can be improved even further when transitions coincide with, follow, or precede a regular event in the child's life. An arbitrary time like 4:30 on Thursdays, for example, is regular and predictable, but may seem entirely random to many children. Worse, it might interrupt a preferred activity. Kids in kindergarten and younger, in particular, seldom have a reliable sense of the day of the week or the actual time of the day. When 4:30 on Thursday happens also to coincide with the end of dance class or the beginning of a favorite family television show, predictability increases. Perhaps the most child-centered formula for predictable

transition gets the kids excited to "get to Dad's house in time for" some desirable family activity.

3. *Buy or create a large, child-friendly wall calendar.* This simple tool can similarly help increase predictability in each home. Before the end of each month, enlist the kids to help color the next month's Dad-days blue and Mom-days green. Use clip-art pictures, stickers, and photos to add other events (birthdays, holidays, and travel) so that the kids can better foresee these activities as well. When the parent-on-duty gets in the habit of crossing out the day just passed each night at bedtime, it's easy for the kids to count down the number of days until the next transition.

4. *The place matters, too.* When transitions occur directly from one caregiver to another, doing so in a predictable and familiar setting can help. The receiving parent's driveway is a common choice, but caregivers who cannot approach (and those who are legally restricted from approaching) their co-parent's home can encourage the kids' compliance with transitions by meeting in a child-friendly and desirable setting. Consider a preferred restaurant with the promise of a reentry meal ahead, an arcade where the kids can spend the tokens they've been earning doing chores, or the mall where older kids can converge with friends before leaving with the receiving parent back to travel to her home.

5. *Bait and bribes.* Neither word suggests sophisticated parenting, but each describes a valuable technique. "Bait" refers to something that lures the child into the transition and helps to minimize focus on the loss/reunion emotions that accompany every

change. For example, tape a pocket or an envelope on the back of the driver's seat, directly in front of where she'll sit on the ride home. When she expects to find a new riddle, joke, drawing, or poem waiting there for her, she'll have another reason to join you with a minimum of fuss.

With older and more mature children, "bait" can also take the shape of a jigsaw puzzle, Lego creation, chess set, or anything that continues one piece at a time toward a distant conclusion. At each arrival, the child and the receiving parent each take one more turn, add one more piece, or select one more component (but no more) blindly from the box of ten thousand components and join it to the slowly evolving whole. This creates a thread of continuity that the child can look forward to across a long period of time.

Bribes are more obviously positives that are offered contingent on behavior success. "If we can get going soon, we'll have time to stop at . . . ," or "If you're buckled in by the time that I count to ten then you can have . . ." There's nothing inherently wrong with bribery (putting aside any commentary about the materialistic society that we share), but beware that you're setting a precedent ("No bribe today? Then I'm not going!"), that inflation is at play ("That was enough last week, but I'm bored of that now. I need more!"), and that your co-parent needs to be in on the scheme from the start, lest you end up in a bidding war for the child's time and attention.

Scripting Separation and Reentry

Just as the adults can script the transition in the interest of decreasing the likelihood that they will bicker in front of the children, the child's departure and reentry can also be scripted.

Separation from the sending parent will be easier when the process is routine. We pack the night before, for example, so that the early morning pickup (or school bus) is not delayed. The sending parent gives a "One hour till Dad gets here!" reminder, and then a five-minute reminder. At the door each child gets five kisses in her palm, a high five, and a piece of (sugar-free) chewing gum for the road. Out the front door, Mom flashes the entry light. Dad honks the horn twice, and off they go.

Reentry can be the reverse. High fives, unload in the garage, and hot chocolate around the kitchen table together before everyone rushes off. With younger children, reentry can be more creative, routinely using a song or poem or story to ease the kids back into the home.

Thinking Through the Resistance

When transition resistance and refusal persist beyond these simple strategies, co-parents need to jointly consider each of a number of possible explanations, keeping in mind that more than one factor may be simultaneously in play:

1. *Is the child only saying what she believes the listener wants to hear?* Kids are highly vulnerable to suggestion. When Dad asks, "You don't want to go with Mom, do you?" he's likely to get a nod

of confirmation no matter how the child actually feels. Co-parents have to be wholeheartedly supportive of the child's relationship with the other parent and completely confident that the child is safe in that other parent's care. The better statement for Dad to make would be, "I can tell that you're nervous, but I know that you guys'll have a great time!"

2. *Does the child resist separation from the sending parent in general?* Normal separation anxiety and the child's fears for the sending parent's well-being in his absence (particularly when that parent is depressed, lonely, or ill, and when the child has been adultified, parentified, or infantilized) can be seen not only in transition resistance and refusal, but in a much broader difficulty separating. Transitional objects can help, but many of these instances cannot be resolved until the sending parent's neediness is otherwise resolved.

3. *Is the child resisting something incidental to the receiving parent?* Surprisingly often, a child's transition resistance is discovered to be a response to the actual experience of moving between homes (the receiving parent's car smells odd or he drives too fast), to others who accompany the receiving parent or share her home (his new girlfriend or parents or roommate), or to the physical environment in which the parent and child spend time (a noisy neighbor or a scary pet). In this situation, the child might not hesitate to leave the sending parent, but probably asks a lot of questions in advance of the transition: "Will Grandma be there, too?" "Is he picking me up on his motorcycle again?" "Do you think he got me a bed yet?" After offering reasonable reassurances and

redirecting the child to talk to the receiving parent directly, it's important that the co-parents discuss the child's questions and the anxiety that might be prompting them.

One important clue lies in how the child engages the receiving parent under other circumstances (after the school play, at swim practice). A warm and eager greeting may suggest that resistance has nothing to do with the relationship and everything to do with these other, incidental factors. Of course, discovering what these specific factors are can open up another can of worms entirely. What should Mom do if she discovers that Billy is allergic to the carpet in the apartment she just leased? Worse, what should Dad do if he discovers that Billy resists transitioning into his care because Dad's new wife's son is Billy's worst enemy at school?

4. *Is the receiving parent sensitive and responsive to the child's needs?* A caregiver's ability to recognize and respond appropriately to a child's needs—the relative "fit" between the two—will determine the quality of their relationship. A child whose experience leads him to believe that the receiving parent is neither sensitive nor responsive will expectably be nervous about transitioning into that parent's care. Identification of parenting deficits on this level (during the course of a GAL investigation, for example) calls for parent training and therapy intended first to assure that the child's needs will be met in that parent's care and, second, to facilitate the child's comfort in that relationship.

5. *Is the receiving parent more strict or demanding than the sending parent?* Co-parenting inconsistencies often play a role in a

child's transition resistance. Who wouldn't resist leaving Disneyland (see Chapter 10) to return to boot camp? The answer to this dilemma is not a bidding war for the child's attention, with each parent enforcing fewer and fewer limits and buying cooler and cooler toys. The answer, once again, is consistency.

This dilemma is sometimes compounded by real and dramatic differences between the two parents' resources, homes, or locations. In these instances, even the best co-parent communication, collaboration, and consistency can fail to diminish the child's transition resistance. One home is still bigger and more exciting than the other. In this case, the answer then becomes a simple matter of firm, calm, and consistent limits voiced in reassuring "we" statements: "I know it's hard to leave, buddy. Your mom and I have talked about it. We know that you'll be fine. You'll be back here in four more nights."

6. *Can the child be gradually weaned (back) into the receiving parent's care?* In those instances in which a child resists transition for no objectively verifiable reason (as when alienation is at work) or when the receiving caregiver is unfamiliar (as when a parent has been unavailable for a long period due to travel, incarceration, or legal restrictions), a rapid but graduated course of contact may be necessary. In both cases, the goal is to facilitate the child's experience of the receiving parent as safe and secure, sensitive and responsive, a little at a time without allowing too long of a period to lapse between contacts. The alienated child may need corrective experiences that dispel inaccurate expectations. The reuniting child may need the opportunity to (re)build

familiarity and comfort. In each case, transition involving a supportive third party (the child's therapist), accompanied by a trusted ally (the child's best friend), or conducted in a supervised setting may further help to diminish the child's resistance.

Chapter 17

Sibling Conflict and Parallel Process

B
rothers and sisters can be a child's greatest source of emotional support.

Over the course of a lifetime, siblings usually have more shared experiences than spouses, more values in common than friends, and longer common memories even than those parents share with their children. Don't let the squabbles called "sibling rivalry" fool you. The sibling bond can be a child's long-term life support system.

In the natural course of development, siblings must conflict. Early on in development, these conflicts are about who will win the parents' affection and attention. The competition shifts later in development to control of material possessions and privileges: who gets the bicycle or the front seat or the last cookie in the cookie jar. Along the way, a million minor quarrels gradually serve the purpose of differentiation. Each child creates a psychological niche within which he can shine apart from the others. One becomes an athlete and another an academic. One turns to art and another to music.

These are among the earliest roots of identity formation, the forces that help each of us to define a sense of self.

For all of the bruises and insults, siblings who successfully differentiate are more likely to maintain a strong relationship later in life. They develop complementary skills and feel less threatened by one another's strengths. They are better prepared to develop their own intimate relationships as adults, confident in each other's support, however dormant and distant it might be.

Healthy co-parents implicitly understand and nurture the differentiation that must occur among their children. The caregiving team reinforces the siblings' bond ("You two watch out for each other") and encourages each child's unique interests. The safety net that they weave together contains the kids not only as growing individuals, but as brothers and sisters, reassuring and setting limits all at once.

Are Healthy Parents "Fair"?

"It's not fair!" is the war cry of childhood and a trap for all but the most thoughtful parents.

"It's not fair" is a child's favorite refrain when the neighbor gets one, and his brother has one, but he does not. It's a guilt trip that unfortunately leverages far too many parents into far too many concessions in the false belief that good parents must somehow distribute the wealth evenly.

Are Healthy Parents "Fair"? *(continued)*

In fact, it is impossible for your kids to have equal shares of everything and every opportunity. Don't even try. Your goal as a healthy parent is not to make sure that Billy gets one for every one that you give Sally. The goal is to see that Billy has what he needs and that Sally has what she needs, even if these are very different.

So what's the best answer to "It's not fair!"?

It's not, "When you're his age you will . . . and when I was your age I had to walk five miles barefoot in the snow . . ." The best answer is, instead, "You're right. It's not fair," and then, having sidestepped the content, you can talk about the feelings: "You sound pretty frustrated . . ."

When co-parents conflict, the natural and necessary process of sibling differentiation and identity formation can be thrown off track. For some sib groups, the process becomes exaggerated. The adult tension and the children's associated insecurity tears them apart, leaving one child clinging to Mom and the other clinging to Dad. Identified with their respective combatants, polarized by the adult battles, perhaps even adultified as each parent's new partner, these siblings' rivalry becomes nothing more than an echo of their parents' war. The kids escalate in parallel with the adults and are likely to end, like their parents, permanently separated, bitter, and scared.

In one typical scenario, the natural process of gender identification prompts Billy to identify with his dad and Sally to identify with her mom. When the adults separate, each child resists transitioning into the care of the opposite-gender parent. When they must be together, Billy and Sally reenact Mom and Dad's battles (a phenomenon psychologists refer to as "parallel process"), even to the extent of mimicking the unfamiliar but threatening-sounding words they overhear.

Billy and Sally's sibling rivalry has been distorted. It is no longer about healthy differentiation and identity formation, but about championing one parent and defeating the other. These children are at risk for far more than their own personal insecurities. Conscripted into the adults' battle, they risk losing each other's support long after their parents have moved on.

And then there are those for whom sibling differentiation stalls when the parents' conflict erupts. It might be delayed for the duration of the parents' conflict or it might die in its tracks, another victim of the adults' selfish battles.

Lacking the security of the adults' limits and support, overwhelmed by the tension in the home, these siblings cling to one another like shipwreck survivors surrounded by sharks. Natural sibling rivalry disappears. One child may be parentified by default or by directive because Mom and Dad are too consumed with their battle to do their jobs right ("Take care of your little sister," or "Now that Dad's gone, you're the man of the family!"). Another child may be infantilized into a complementary role. The kids become cemented together in these new and distorted mutual dynamics in order to cope with their immediate reality. A war is being waged all around them. Mom and Dad are too short-tempered and unpredictable and overwhelmed to do their jobs as parents.

"We've got to take care of each other."

This childhood coping strategy comes at a cost. These siblings might never adequately differentiate. Each child's identity becomes enmeshed with that of the other. What was once an adaptive coping mechanism outlives its usefulness to become an adult hindrance and even pathology. Brother and sister may never quite escape their learned childhood roles as pseudocaregiver and child. They find themselves too anxious to be apart and unable to develop healthy intimate relationships away from one another. Their prospective partners are put off by the constant connection between the two. They have each other, but few if any other connections to the world.

These distorted sibling dynamics are obvious to all but the most overwhelmed and self-centered caregivers. Healthy co-parents realize there's something wrong when the kids argue constantly about "'dultry,'" rather than about donuts and about "cheating" even when there's no board game between them. Healthy co-parents recognize that the kids are repeating expletives they could only have overheard in their home, and that punishing the kids for these behaviors is the height of hypocrisy.

Healthy co-parents are able look out from under the weight of their adult conflict and wonder why the kids aren't arguing like they used to, why they seem oddly clingy to one another, and why neither wants to leave the house without the other. True, this one is harder to see. Like the chameleon child, this dysfunction is quiet and even desirable in its unobtrusiveness. But healthy co-parents will see it and wonder what's going on.

But there's the rub: co-parents who are healthy enough to recognize their children's distress are healthy enough not to cause it in the first place.

The answer here, as always, is to keep the kids out of the middle, to separate the adult conflict from the co-parenting collaboration, always putting the kids' needs first. Healthy co-parents remain committed to meeting the children's needs, to communicating constructively, and to maintaining consistency and structure in the kids' best interests. When healthy co-parents separate, the parenting plan must preserve and nurture the sibling relationship, recognizing the support that the kids find in each others' presence despite their bickering and arguments to the contrary. This is inevitably a balancing act, a compromise that accounts for each child's individual needs and that of the sibling group as a whole. (The role of the sibling relationship in creating a parenting plan is discussed in Chapter 12.)

Chapter 18

Introducing New Partners and Co-Parents

S ooner or later, conflicted adults may find new partners. Sometimes the new partner comes first, sparking a critical conflict or revealing a schism long buried and ignored. Other times the new partner comes later, an estranged or separated or divorced adult's port in the storm, a new love, hearthmate, or significant other.

All too often this sequence of events is blurred and contested. She says he was having an affair all along. He defends that they only got together after he moved out. He says that she's cheating on him, and she responds that they're only friends.

The passions that accompany this argument are understandably intense. At issue are matters that cut deep to the core of most people: trust and adequacy, loyalty and betrayal, privacy and exposure. Add to this the powerful threats that arise when the relationship includes physical intimacy—STDs, HIV, AIDS—and the adult relationship becomes a powder keg that can explode at any time, anywhere, even in front of the kids.

This book does not take a position about the moral, ethical, or religious values that often frame these conflicts. Such perspectives are yours to determine with the help of your chosen advisors and friends. This book is, however, intensely concerned with the health and well-being of children, and this subject—if and how and when to introduce new partners—may be most adults' greatest challenge when it comes to keeping kids out of the middle.

Children as Conspirators and Spies

Here's how to hurt your children:

"Shhh! Don't tell Mommy. This is private."

"Hey buddy, who's that lady over at Dad's house?"

"This is our secret, okay?"

"What happens in this house stays in this house!"

"If you tell Daddy about this, he'll cry and cry."

"I'll get you that toy after you tell me about what happens at Mom's house."

"If you talk about this, you will never play another video game in this house ever again."

These are among the painfully familiar, selfish manipulations that parents use to enlist their children as spies and conspirators in their adult war. These deceits, bribes, and threats can be used more or less successfully when kids are exposed to a parent's drug or alcohol use, absence and neglect, illegal actions, physical and sexual abuse, or illicit affair. But putting your kids in the middle in this way is not only destructive, it's stupid. It's like trying to carry water in a paper bag.

It may work briefly but will inevitably leak and then fall apart entirely.

Putting your kids in the middle in this way is adultification taken to a new height. The kids might experience the hush-hush exclusive connection with one parent as an exciting promotion ("Mom's trusting me!") until the expectable pressures and the implicit betrayal kick in ("What if Dad asks . . . ?"). Then any fleeting sense of specialness disappears. In its place grows monstrous guilt, anger, and fear, topped by the credible certainty that she is responsible for her parents' conflict.

But you wonder, "What's wrong with asking my kids to keep a secret?"

The answer is nothing at all, unless the secret aligns the child with one family member and against another. The child's experience of divided loyalties, her fears of betrayal, and her compelling need to win both parents' affection and attention make this kind of secret not only destructive, but doomed to failure. Asking your child to keep a secret from her other parent is adultifying, at least, and alienating as often as not. No matter the wording, no matter the threat or promise, the message is ultimately this: "Shhh! It's you and me against your other parent."

Surprises are different. A surprise is knowledge shared between a parent and a child that is intended to please the other parent and is intended to be shared (hopefully soon, because the paper bag will start to leak very quickly!). In place of pressures, threats, and deceits, surprises are accompanied by giggles, pleasure, and excitement. A surprise can be anything from a holiday present, a birthday surprise, or even breakfast in bed.

"Okay. If there's to be no secrets," you're wondering, "then why can't I ask my kids about their other parent?"

Because your pointed and intrusive questions can create as much pressure about telling as secrets create about not telling. There's a difference, of course, between an innocuous, "Did you and Mom have fun this weekend?" and a demanding, "Did your dad's friend sleep over? In whose bed? Was she there in the morning?"

Talking to Your Kids When They Return

So what should I ask my child after he's spent time with my co-parent?

You're the receiving parent. Your kids have been away in their other parent's care for several days. The schedule has been in place long enough now that everyone's used to it and coping pretty well. You've learned to dilute your longing for the kids by working long hours and catching up on housework while they're gone, giving you more time to be there for them when you become the parent-on-duty.

You pick them up at your co-parent's apartment or in the carpool line after school, or you greet them in your doorway as their other parent drives off. Hugs. Kisses. Maybe you have a reentry ritual, or maybe all you get is an urgent, "Hey, I need ten dollars for . . ." and a whiny, "Can I go to . . . ?" and then the transition is over, the kids disappear to play or do homework or return to their preferred digital reality. Or maybe you get some time together driving back home, on the way to lacrosse practice or cuddling together before bed.

Talking to Your Kids When They Return *(continued)*

No matter how curious or concerned you are, don't put the kids on the spot with focused, leading questions about their other home. These questions need to be directed to your co-parent.

Ask, instead, about the relationships and events that create a continuous thread across their two homes. Ask about the members of the soccer team or Billy's lab partner in science class. Ask how play practice is going and how far she's gotten in the novel she started last month. Ask about his karate instructor and how black-belt training is coming.

Do not ask about your co-parent. Do not ask about your co-parent's home or friends or parenting practices. Do not ask about your co-parent's new lover or new car or new swing set. Do not enlist your child as your spy.

These subjects will come up, of course, in the natural course of conversation. You ask about choir rehearsal, and Billy offers that dad's new girlfriend drove him there. You ask about a social studies project, and Sally mentions that she started working on it on Mom's really cool new computer.

Take a deep breath. Take notes in your head: New girlfriend? How did she afford a new computer? Do not respond to these tantalizing and provocative tidbits. These details are grist for co-parenting communication. This is not permission for probing the child's incidental reference to something that you find provocative. Your best path, instead, is a supportive "Okay," and a conscious effort to get back on a child-centered track.

Talking to Your Kids When They Return *(continued)*

respond to these tantalizing and provocative tidbits. These
details are grist for co-parenting communication. This is not permission for probing the child's incidental reference to something that you find provocative. Your best path, instead, is a
supportive, "Okay," and a conscious effort to get back on a
child-centered track.

Introductions, Shared Time, and Sleepovers

When should the kids meet your new friend?

How should you introduce her?

What should they be told? When and how and by whom?

Pace yourself and your kids. Everyone should respect that the days
and weeks and months after the adult separation are a time of adjustment. You and your children will more or less subtly renegotiate your
relationship. Limits will be tested. Roles will be redefined. With so
much up in the air—a new home, new routines, new boundaries, missing the absent parent—adding a new significant other to the mix is a
bad idea. It's a bit like hanging the pictures before the paint dries on the
walls.

So how long should you wait?

There's no formula for determining when best to introduce a new
partner to your kids, but if there were, it would take into account how

much adult conflict the kids have endured and for how long; whether there have been separations and reunions before, and how many and how recently; and how much has actually changed in the kids' lives as a result of the separation.

It is reasonable to guess that kids might adjust more quickly when they have experienced a minimum of conflict spanning a brief period with no prior separation/reunion cycles and a minimum of change. Conversely, kids who have endured intense conflict for most of their lives—multiple back-and-forth adult separations and reunions and enormous practical change (relocating several times, changing schools, loss of friends)—may take a very long time to settle in.

Alert your co-parent first. This is a good general rule any time anything significant occurs in your life that bears on the children. Alerted, your co-parent will be more likely to respond to the kids' otherwise unexpected and spontaneous comments ("Did you know that Daddy got his nose pierced?") calmly. Without advance notice, even the most well-meaning and cooperative co-parent can be startled into a reaction ("He did *what*?!") which colors the kids' feelings ("Mom thinks that your nose ring is stupid!").

"But if I alert him, then he'll tell the kids first, before I'm ready!"

Then you probably shouldn't tell your co-parent before you're ready for the kids to know, too. Timing is everything. Tell her the day before you plan to talk to the kids. Tell her in an e-mail sent just before she arrives to drop off the kids, knowing that she'll get it upon her return home and can digest it before the kids return to her care. Tell her in a note that is exchanged adult-to-adult at the next transition, which she can read after the transition and be ready for the kids' return later.

What should you say? Alerting your co-parent to your new relationship is not about asking permission. It is not flaunting the fact that you're moving on and (*nah-nah, nah-nah-nah!*) she hasn't yet. It does not require divulging details. It's just a simple heads-up that might sound at a minimum like this: "FYI: I'm dating. His name is Ron. The kids will meet him this weekend."

Don't lie to your children. "Who's that, Mommy?" Not only is lying a terrible example for the kids to copy and the height of hypocrisy for most of us, it almost never succeeds. Your shoot-from-the-hip, "He's just a friend," excuse might manage the moment, but little more. No doubt the lie will come back to haunt you later when the kids discover that he's more than just a friend. The result will be a loss of trust (at a time when they've already lost a lot) and unnecessary anger (when they've already got a lot to be angry about). The result may also be resentment toward your new partner that unfairly colors the kids' perceptions for a very long time to come.

Be proactive. Plan ahead. Your new partner is a big deal to the kids. Pretending that the kids won't notice or don't care or rationalizing that who you date is no one's business but your own is selfish and shortsighted. The kids do care and will notice, and it is their business as soon as they have to share your time, attention, affection, and space. Better to pave the way in advance.

How? Start with the script that defines the end of the intimate adult relationship (see Chapter 9) and add a new chapter: ". . . and some day, Mommy might find a new grown-up to love, and Daddy might find a new grown-up to love, but we will always love you no matter what."

The Physics of Love

Keep in mind that children tend to think in black-and-white, all-or-nothing terms. In your child's view, your love is as finite as the coffee in your cup or the number of M&Ms in a bag. The more that you give to an intimate adult partner, the less that they will get.

Your child probably thinks of his own capacity for love in similar terms. If he gives some to your new partner, he fears that he won't have enough left for his other parent. This is often heard in a child's eventual confession, "If I love Mommy's new husband, then I can't love Daddy, too!"

We must teach our kids that love is infinite, that everyone has more love to give than there is sand on the beach. "Wouldn't it be cool," you ask, "if every sip you take of your chocolate milk made twice as much as in your cup? Love works the same way. The more that you give, the more that you've got."

Introduce your partner when she's ready to develop a relationship with your children (and not before). Are you a parent even when you don't have your kids? Even when you're not the parent-on-duty?

If the answer is no, if you believe that you're only a parent when you're the parent-on-duty, then you're at risk for developing a relationship that is incompatible with your kids' needs. You might find a new partner who is fun, exciting, loving, and wonderful, but who is not ready to share you with your kids. Introducing your kids to this partner is an invitation to feeling split in two, to the kids feeling marginalized and angry, and to your new partner sooner or later forcing you to choose between the adult relationship and the parenting relationship.

This is not a partner whom the kids should ever meet.

But if your answer is yes, if you are a parent 24/7/365, if meeting a new partner includes accepting everything in your lives, including your children, then you're likely to develop a relationship with someone who will someday be ready to meet the kids.

Sharing Your Kids with Your Co-Parent's Partner

Even if you genuinely don't care that your former intimate partner has moved on, even if you're pleased that the kids like his new girlfriend, and even if you think that she might be a reasonable human being, the idea that she might be taking care of *your* children instead of you can be infuriating!

Here's how it happens: the kids are over at Dad's house. His new girlfriend is there, too. They eat supper together, but he has to run out to an evening meeting or to the grocery store or to the gym for an hour. The girlfriend and the kids get along just fine. Technically he could bring them to you for the hour, but it's a twenty-minute drive each way, and everyone has already acknowledged that transitions back and forth are stressful for the kids, so the girlfriend becomes the parent-on-duty.

Maybe that's okay. It's only for an hour.

The next week, Billy has swim practice at the same time that Sally has dance. Why not divide and conquer? Dad takes Billy, and his significant other takes Sally. After class, the girls go shopping together to "bond." The next thing you know, your daughter comes home all excited, "Daddy's girlfriend took me out for the day, and I got my nails done, and we went out to lunch, and look at the new shirt she bought me!"

Deep breath.

Firm, calm, and consistent.

Don't fall into the trap. Your daughter needs to share her excitement and receive your implicit reassurance that she's not somehow betraying you by enjoying Dad's new girlfriend. She does *not* need to hear your feelings about how manicures are a mother's job or how you just bought her three new blouses or how you sat home alone all that day (lonely, in the dark and the cold . . .) and how you could have taken her shopping yourself! She does *not* need to hear your thoughts about how Dad and his girlfriend are trying to buy her love, or about how her dad never let *you* spend money like that back when you were together!

Deep breath.

Firm, calm, and consistent.

These many powerful feelings belong in your journal or in a conversation with your best friend over coffee or in your therapist's office. In some more constructive form they might have a place in a communication directed to your co-parent. But voicing any of these to your child (even letting them show on your face) risks putting her in the middle.

Deep breath.

Firm, calm, and consistent.

"That's wonderful, sweetie! I think that shirt will go just right with your . . ."

The fact is, you can't control what goes on in your co-parent's home. He can share his parenting responsibilities any way that he chooses so long as the kids are safe. He can hire babysitters or nannies or enroll the kids in classes. He can arrange his parenting time so that he does little or no parenting himself.

He can bring a new significant other into the home every week. He can introduce the kids to the partner-du-jour and even leave them in her care, so long as they're safe.

You can, too.

Hopefully, neither of you would do these things because you know that, even though the kids are safe, they need structure. They need stability. They need the love and attention and affection from you, their parents.

And if you believe that your co-parent is introducing your kids to his partners too soon or too often? If you believe that the kids are missing him because he's busy or absent even when he's the parent-on-duty? All that you can do—and the best that you can do—is to try to bring it to his attention without blame or accusation. Don't say, "Why did you . . . ?" or "I can't believe that you . . . !"

Try, instead, "I wonder if . . . ?" or "Can we talk about . . . ?"

The Right of First Refusal

Chapter 12 introduced the idea that co-parents should plan ahead for those unanticipated situations that make a parent unavailable for her usual residential responsibilities. The "right of first refusal" is a contingency which allows that the POD's co-parent will have the first option to assume parenting responsibilities if the parent-on-duty must be absent for more than a specific period of time. For example:

"If the POD will be unavailable to provide direct care to the children for a period of twenty-four hours or longer, then the other parent will be asked to serve as POD before any other potential caregivers are queried."

Does this contingency meet the children's needs? The answer will depend on the child and the circumstance. In some instances, the right of first refusal serves the adults' needs and can actually become an impediment to the children's comfort with their parents' new partners.

Joining the Co-Parenting Team

If the goal is genuinely to work together to understand and better meet the children's needs, then the co-parenting team should include "all the adults who participate in caring for a child." Yes, this does mean that once Mom's boyfriend and Dad's mother step into the parent-on-duty role, they should be considered part of the co-parenting team.

Does this mean that our weekly breakfast meetings should include them? That our transition reports and e-mail communications should be copied to them? Does this mean that we need to consult them about which camp to send the kids to and how to pay for orthodontia and about bedtimes and privileges?

Yes. There's no reason that child-centered caregivers wouldn't share their communications with everyone invested in the kid's care. Putting aside all of the complicated adult emotions and territoriality, the more caregivers who are involved, the more information and support will be available and the stronger the kids' safety net will be.

But are all co-parents created equal? No.

Dad and his new wife are in charge when it comes to decisions in their home. They keep Mom in the loop in the interest of consistency and because they value her view of the kids, but Mom takes a backseat in these decisions. Mom and Dad may be jointly in charge when it comes to major life decisions for the kids, and each might choose to include their respective partners, but ultimately these partners take a backseat to the legal decision makers.

Can you demand that your co-parent not include her new partner in the process? No. And neither can she make any similar demand of you.

Chapter 19

A Dictionary of Dilemmas

The world would be a simpler place if relationships were rational, logical enterprises and feelings were subject to the laws of physics. In such an analytical world, we'd be able to plot a straightforward course through life. We'd be able to raise our children with much greater certainty about their futures. And we'd be a passionless species.

The same intense emotions and irrational relationships that can make our lives so complicated and painful also make our lives full of incredible beauty and potential. In the depths of agony and despair, confusion and loneliness, it's easy to wish for simplicity, but if that wish were ever granted, the cost would be far greater than the benefit.

Better than wishing for a passionless existence, as healthy parents we must learn to feed our children from the part of the cup that is half full. We must find joy, pleasure, pride, success, and opportunity everywhere that we can, learning to cope with the pain and hurt and anger, failure and crisis and fear as well prepared as possible.

For every guideline and recommendation about co-parenting addressed in this book, there are at least a hundred exceptions and several million permutations. It may be that every page prompts some parent, somewhere, to say, "Yes, but what about . . . ?" That's what your trusted pediatrician and preferred mental health provider, your own parents and clergy, and your best friend and neighbor are for. They are the ones with whom you can talk through the exceptions, stretch the guidelines, and bend the rules wherever necessary to fit your kids' particular needs.

There are, however, a handful of special cases in need of a final word or two. These are dilemmas that are common enough to deserve attention, however brief.

Two Adults/One Parent?

This looks good on paper, but seldom works.

Two adults enjoy a mutually rewarding intimate relationship, and then a child enters the picture. An unexpected or an unwanted pregnancy, a former partner's death or disappearance, a new court order, a generous offer to serve as someone's godparent, and life changes abruptly.

Enter a child, stage left.

The dilemma arises when one adult accepts the responsibility to become a parent, but the other does not. Either the two make an explicit agreement that only one will do the parenting, or, in the natural course of conflict and crisis, the same outcome is achieved even though it's never been discussed.

In theory, it sounds like a simple situation. The child learns to go to Dad when he's hungry or tired or needs to borrow the car because Dad's partner doesn't do those things. Call it a division of labor. So what's the problem?

In practice, this triangle of relationships is terribly unbalanced and likely to break. Dad feels torn between his intimate partner and his child, constantly trying to serve two masters. Sometimes the adult partner and the child compete for his attention and affection; sometimes they gang up together, and he feels like he has two kids on his hands. Either way, he has no co-parenting support.

And how does this affect the child? Dad's partner makes the child feel unimportant and like an unwelcome guest or an intruder. The child wonders why he's unloved or ignored and why Dad sometimes chooses the other adult over him. He's likely to try to split between the two, trying to break up the adult relationship or, failing that, to get himself adultified so the three can manage their relationship as peers.

Try as you might, this two-adults/one-parent dilemma is a recipe for disaster. Better to restrict the intimate adult relationship to your own time, when you're not serving as parent-on-duty, or to build a relationship with a genuine partner, someone who will complement and support you in every part of your life.

Relationship Ambivalence and Ambiguity: A "Trial" Separation?

It is entirely reasonable to expect that the prospect of ending an intimate adult relationship brings up powerful mixed feelings. "Yes, I want out!" collides with, "No, don't leave me alone!" and conflicts with, "Get out, I can't stand it anymore!" which gives way to, "Come back, I can't live without you!"

The result can be a back-and-forth cycle of separations and reunions that might not matter at all, if it weren't for the kids.

This cycle of conflict/separation/reunion wreaks havoc on a child's psyche. It upsets every bit of consistency and stability and predictability, the structure upon which her fragile self is being built. Perhaps the only thing worse than grieving over the loss associated with parents' separation is grieving and then discovering that it was all unnecessary and then not knowing next time whether to grieve again.

So what's a caring parent supposed to do? Staying together for the kids isn't right (see Chapter 8). Separating needlessly makes even less sense!

One way to deal with this dilemma is to agree to a trial separation.

Rather than putting the kids through the impassioned and unpredictable revolving door of separations and reunions, a trial separation is a planned and predictable process. By structuring it, everyone's anxiety is diminished, and the kids will be better able to cope with the process. Here's how:

1. A trial separation requires that the adult couple be actively involved in some kind of counseling. A neutral third party will

help to keep the process child-centered and sensible. It is routinely important for each adult to simultaneously have a separate therapist to help sort through the intense emotions and difficult decisions ahead.

2. Do the kids also need therapy? Perhaps. Start by keeping the couple's therapist current on the kids' behavior and by maintaining close contact with teachers and other caregivers along the way. A therapist can become an important emotional anchor for a child throughout the course of change.

3. The separation and all that follows must be predictable and the kids kept informed as far in advance as best suits their needs and abilities. This includes a clear and concrete (even if temporary) parenting plan, so the kids know where they'll be and when they'll see each parent, and so they are reassured that all of the details that are important to them are covered.

4. The separation is predetermined to last until a specific date. Six weeks? Six months? Choose an interval that will give you enough time to work intensely with the couple's counselor toward your highest priorities for change. Guarantee the kids that nothing will change between now and then.

5. Agree up front that you will not get involved in another intimate relationship during the trial period.

6. At the end of the trial period, you'll mutually choose one of three options: (a) enough change has occurred that you've decided to reunite; (b) not enough change has occurred, and you've decided to permanently separate; or (c) you're still not sure, so you're agreeing to extend the trial until a specific future date. Make

certain that the outcome is uniformly presented as a "we" statement (see Chapter 10) when you present it to the kids, even if it's not your first choice.

Children and Discretion: Sophie's Other Choice

In William Styron's powerful 1979 novel, *Sophie's Choice*, a mother must choose between her two children, an utterly tragic impossibility.

In the context of co-parent conflict, separation, and divorce, children are often forced to choose between their parents. These are the situations in which they are put in the middle, burdened with a choice that is no less tragic and impossible than Sophie's. The tectonic pressures of trying to please each of two conflicted parents, fears of betrayal and rejection, abandonment and anger, punishment and loss, the dynamics of adultification and parentification, infantilization and alienation together can crush a child.

True, the law in some states allows that some children might choose between their parents. True, a more emotionally mature child caught in between two relatively low-conflict parents might be better able to tolerate these pressures than a less mature child caught between highly conflicted caregivers. But on balance, the best answer is don't.

Don't force your kids to choose between their parents.

Don't fool yourself into thinking that by giving him a choice, you're making him happy. Our job as parents is to help our kids be healthy.

The Poststepparent Dilemma

Mom and Dad marry and together have a bouncing baby boy they name Brutus.

Mom and Dad separate, then divorce.

Mom remarries. Brutus migrates between two homes and, over the years, develops loving relationships with each of three parents: Dad and Mom and Stepdad.

Now Mom and Stepdad separate and divorce. Stepdad has no legal relationship to Brutus. Dad never liked Mom's new husband, and now Mom doesn't like him either. The only thing that Mom and Dad agree about is that Brutus should not see Stepdad any longer. But Stepdad argues on his own behalf that he's very important to the boy.

What to do?

A child-centered process would at least give the child and the estranged stepparent a chance to say good-bye together. They might be encouraged to exchange transitional objects and perhaps even encouraged to exchange holiday cards or birthday presents. The separation should probably be scripted to make certain that no one is blamed for the loss, particularly the child himself.

In some ideal world, Brutus and his stepfather would be allowed to remain in touch. Maybe one Sunday a month at the ballpark and supper out now and again. Awkward and tenuous as this may be, there's no reason that the child should suffer for the adults' conflicts and mistakes. If the stepparent provides the child with another emotional anchor, why take it away?

What About "Makeup Time"?

This is not about planning ahead to be certain that your teenage daughter has long enough to apply mascara and lip gloss. "Makeup time" refers to the complicated arithmetic that fuels many co-parent conflicts when one parent misses out on her usual time with the child. Makeup time is the compensatory period that parent may claim is owed to her as a result.

Examples range from the rational to the ridiculous.

On the one hand, if Dad requests an extended weekend so that he can take Sally camping, it might be reasonable to arrange that Mom could soon thereafter have an extended weekend of her own with Sally. On the other hand, if Mom complains that Billy's play rehearsal ran late, so she didn't get her time with the child and should therefore be allowed to keep him later, it's clear that Mom's needs are at issue, not the child's.

In general, makeup time arrangements are not a good idea. They encourage parent-centered decisions and picayune timekeeping, and they can create a domino effect of compensations for compensations that breeds huge confusion, at the least. Particularly when co-parents communicate and cooperate poorly, makeup time allowances breed conflict that only harms the child.

Perhaps the most important argument against makeup time compensations is the child's need for structure. From the child's perspective, two schedule disruptions is just twice as disruptive. It is seldom the case that the second somehow "makes up" for the first.

When a Parent Cannot Parent

Finally, there are those dilemmas that cannot be resolved, situations in which a child's or an adult's deepest needs and desires cannot be fulfilled. One such dilemma is that of the parent who cannot parent.

Locked out by an angry and disturbed co-parent, disenfranchised by the legal system after years of blood and sweat and tears, or unable to locate a child who has been relocated or even abducted by a selfish caregiver, there are some parents who cannot parent.

All that is left for this parent is grief and that glimmer of distant hope that must not die. In the interest of that faint hope, the parent who cannot parent can create a record of his life, thoughts, dreams, and wishes that his child might someday receive (read about creating a "future album" in Chapter 9). They can create a journal written in the form of "Dear Billy . . ." or "Dear Sally . . ." letters, a collection of birthday and holiday cards that should have been delivered, a photo album recreating events and introducing people who might otherwise have been enjoyed.

When all the legal appeals and private detectives have been exhausted, the parent who cannot parent must grieve the loss and find some way to move forward with his life, accumulating a record of that life as a gift that might someday much later be received by a curious and grateful child.

Resources

H ealthy parenting and co-parenting requires strong advocacy on behalf of your child. Keeping abreast of the many resources and opportunities available will open doors that others believe are locked shut. Speaking out, attending meetings, and doing the research are no longer optional. They are essential to your child's well-being.

The resources listed below are only a representative sample. It would be impossible to compile a comprehensive list and to keep it current. These should only be places to start looking for answers. You must develop the skills and the willingness to talk to friends, neighbors, professionals, politicians, administrators, and executives to find more.

American Bar Association, Section of Family Law

www.abanet.org/family

Learn more about the ethics, practices, and resources that bear on divorce in the United States.

About the new role referred to variously as "parenting coordinator" or "special master":

www.afccnet.org/pdfs/AFCCGuidelinesforParentingcoordinationnew.pdf

American Psychological Association

www.apa.org

Provides valuable information about mental health and child and family development. Start here to discover how to reach your state's psychological association for referral information and local resources.

Association of Family and Conciliation Courts (AFCC)

www.afccnet.org

An international organization leading concerned mental health and family law professionals in developing more child-centered solutions to family conflict, separation, and divorce.

Dr. Garber's Website

www.healthyparent.com

Provides a broad range of resources, links, and services for parents and children.

International Academy of Collaborative Professionals

www.collaborativepractice.com

One of several national and international resources promoting collaborative law. See also www.collaborativedivorce.com and www.collaborativelawnh.org.

The National Domestic Violence Hotline

www.ndvh.org

Phone: 1-800-799-SAFE (7233) or TTY: 1-800-787-3224

From their website: "Help is available to callers 24 hours a day, 365 days a year. Hotline advocates are available for victims and anyone calling on their behalf to provide crisis intervention, safety planning, information, and referrals to agencies in all fifty states, Puerto Rico and the U.S. Virgin Islands. Assistance is available in English and Spanish with access to more than 140 languages through interpreter services."

There are hundreds of valuable resources concerned with divorce. Among these are:

www.divorcesupport.com

www.divorcesource.com

/aacap.org/cs/root/facts_for_families/children_and_divorce

National Register of Health Service Providers in Psychology

www.nationalregister.org

Maintains an international credentialing database and referral resource for mental health services.

Child Find of America

www.childfindofamerica.org

Phone: 1-800-I-am-lost

Provides parents with identification materials that can be registered with the local police department in case a child is lost or taken.

Co-parenting calendars and communication tools:

www.ourfamilywizard.com

www.sharekids.com

www.womansdivorce.com/parenting-plan-calendar.html

www.coparentpro.com

Co-Parenting and Divorce Books

Cooperative Parenting and Divorce: A Parent Guide to Effective Co-Parenting, Susan Blyth Boyan and Ann Marie Termini (Active Parenting, 1999).

Coparenting During and After Divorce: A Handbook for Parents (*Family Advocate* Vol. 30, No. 1), American Bar Association.

The Co-Parenting Survival Guide, Elizabeth Thayer and Jeffrey Zimmerman (New Harbinger, 2001).

Dinosaurs Divorce: A Guide for Changing Families (Dino Life Guides for Families Series), Laurene Krasny Brown and Marc Brown (Little, Brown, 1988).

Mom's House, Dad's House: Making Two Homes for Your Child, Isolina Ricci (Fireside, 1997).

Index

About the Author

Benjamin D. Garber, Ph.D., is a New Hampshire–licensed psychologist, a state-certified guardian ad litem, an active parenting coordinator, and a nationally recognized speaker and writer for legal and mental health publications and the popular press. He is the creator, founder, president, chief executive officer, secretary, administrator, and the only employee (as of press time) of HealthyParent.com, a web-based resource serving the needs of parents like you and the professionals who serve your children.

Dr. Garber is a student of human development by training and has become a family systems proponent through trial and error. His work and the contents of this book emphasize an understanding of how individuals grow over time and the social and emotional context in which these changes occur. Dr. Garber's belief is that it is impossible to adequately understand and respond to any person's needs without a perspective on the course of that person's growth and the relationships within which he or she lives.

Dr. Garber's focus as a therapist, as a consultant to other clinicians, to attorneys, and to the courts, and as a writer and speaker for more than a quarter of a century has been on understanding and meeting

children's needs. He believes there is no more challenging and rewarding task than helping conflicted caregivers learn how to put aside their
own difficulties and improve their skills in order to better serve their
children.

For more information go to www.healthyparent.com or contact
the author at papaben@healthyparent.com.

About HealthyParent.com

HealthyParent.com is Dr. Garber's website and your gateway to keeping kids out of the middle. Created in 1999, HealthyParent.com provides caregivers and professionals alike an incomparable breadth and depth of child-centered information.

Click on CHILDREN AND DIVORCE to learn more about the impact that co-parental conflict, separation and divorce often has on children and how to minimize those destructive outcomes. Learn about alienation as a natural and necessary family dynamic and as a weapon that some caregivers use against one another. Learn about how family stress is easily and often mistaken for problems including ADD and ADHD and how to avoid this destructive misunderstanding.

Click on ABOUT PSYCHOTHERAPY IN GENERAL to learn about how to find the best mental health resources available for yourself and your children, what types of psychotherapy to consider, and how to introduce the idea of psychotherapy to a child.

Click on WHICH HAT TO WEAR? in order to better understand the many and varied roles that mental health professionals can play in the process of assisting your child. What is a Guardian ad litem? A custody evaluator? A parenting coordinator? What is family therapy as opposed to sibling therapy or individual therapy?

Click on DR. GARBER'S PROFESSIONAL PUBLICATIONS to read many of the articles referenced through this book and to find links to other, related professional and mass media publications on related subjects.

Make www.HealthyParent.com the next step along the path to raising healthier children.